# THE WEST MIDLAND LINES OF THE GWR

# THE WEST MIDLAND LINES OF THE GWR

## Keith M. Beck

LONDON

**IAN ALLAN LTD**

First published 1983

ISBN 0 7110 1211 3



Published by Ian Allan Ltd, Shepperton, Surrey;
and printed by Ian Allan Printing Ltd at their works
at Coombelands in Runnymede, England

## Dedication

**To the memory of my late grandfather,
Elisha Maylott: sometime Chief Clerk,
Locomotive, Carriage & Wagon
Department, Worcester**

# Contents

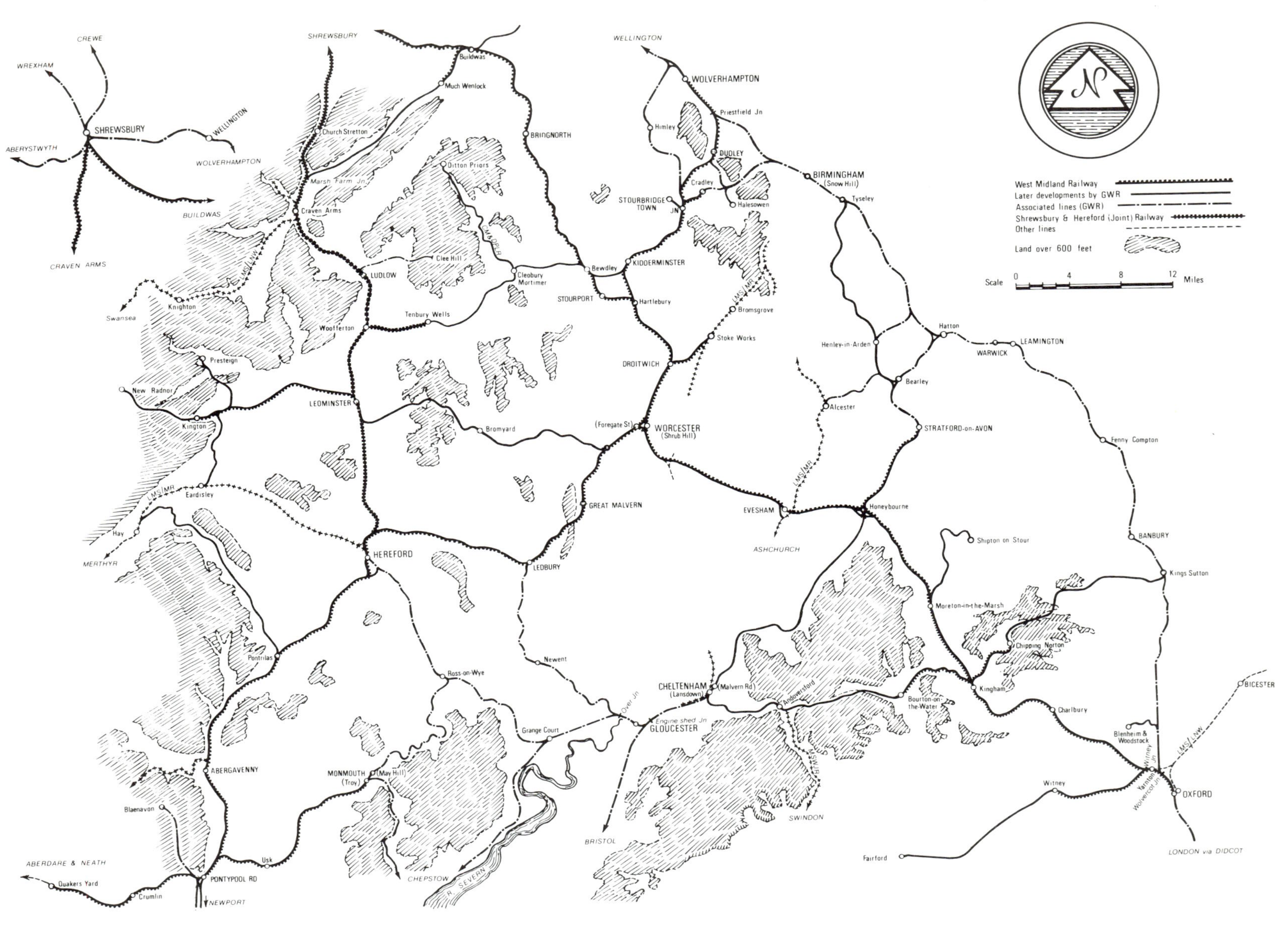

West Midland Railway
Later developments by GWR
Associated lines (GWR)
Shrewsbury & Hereford (Joint) Railway
Other lines
Land over 600 feet
Scale
Miles
0   4   8   12
BICESTER
OXFORD
LONDON via DIDCOT
LMS/LNW
Wolvercot Jn
Blenheim & Woodstock
Kings Sutton
Chipping Norton
Darlbury
Witney
BANBURY
Kingham
Fenny Compton
Shipton on Stour
Moreton-in-the-Marsh
Bourton-on-the-Water
Fairford
LEAMINGTON
WARWICK
Hatton
Bearley
STRATFORD-on-AVON
Honeybourne
MSWJR
SWINDON
Alderbury
BIRMINGHAM (Snow Hill)
Tyseley
Henley-in-Arden
Alcester
LMS/MR
EVESHAM
ASHCHURCH
CHELTENHAM (Lansdown)
Engine shed Jn
GLOUCESTER
WOLVERHAMPTON
Priestfield Jn
DUDLEY
Halesowen
Cradley
Himley
LMS/SW
Bromsgrove
Stoke Works
WORCESTER (Shrub Hill)
DROITWICH
Over Jn
BRISTOL
WELLINGTON
STOURBRIDGE TOWN
JN
KIDDERMINSTER
Hartlebury
Bewdley
STOURPORT
(Foregate St)
GREAT MALVERN
Malvern Rd
Newent
Grange Court
CHEPSTOW
R. SEVERN
BRIDGNORTH
Cleobury Mortimer
CM&DPLR
LEDBURY
Ross-on-Wye
MONMOUTH (Troy)
May Hill
Buildwas
Much Wenlock
Ditton Priors
Clee Hill
Tenbury Wells
Bromyard
HEREFORD
SHREWSBURY
Church Stretton
Marsh Farm Jn
Craven Arms
LUDLOW
Woofferton
LEOMINSTER
Pontrilas
ABERGAVENNY
Usk
PONTYPOOL RD
NEWPORT
MN/SW
Knighton
Presteign
Kington
Eardisley
LMS/MR
Blaenavon
Crumlin
CREWE
WREXHAM
ABERYSTWYTH
WELLINGTON
WOLVERHAMPTON
BUILDWAS
Knighton
Swansea
New Radnor
Hay
MERTHYR
CRAVEN ARMS
ABERDARE & NEATH
Quakers Yard

# Introduction

Alone among the Great Western Railway's Service Time Tables, No 15 not only listed the principal stations — in this instance, Oxford, Worcester & Wolverhampton — on its cover, but also bore the title 'West Midland Section'. Both descriptions of its contents were a reminder of some of the most troubled days in the entire history of the GWR, for the Oxford, Worcester & Wolverhampton Railway was a 'thorn in the flesh' of much greater magnitude than might have been supposed from the length of its line and the limitations of its resources, while its later days were spent under the title of the West Midland Railway. It was as though the GWR was unable to forget that period of strife and its consequences — which included the arrival of standard gauge rails at Paddington some years earlier than might otherwise have been the case.

Although the Oxford, Worcester & Wolverhampton, perhaps better known in its day as the 'Old Worse and Worse', was the chief constituent of the West Midland Railway, it was only part of that system. Of almost equal importance was the Newport, Abergavenny & Hereford Railway, with its access to the coalfields of Monmouthshire, and the line which not only joined it to the 'Old Worse and Worse', but which was the prime cause of the union which resulted in the West Midland Railway, the Worcester & Hereford Railway. The West Midland shared with the GWR and LNWR the joint ownership of the Shrewsbury & Hereford Railway, a line whose story and fortunes were closely associated with the West Midland — both as a Railway and a Section of the GWR; while several smaller lines were worked by it, and two cross-country routes grew out of its original two branches.

The West Midland Section had no great claim to fame, though it did link three cathedral cities (a fact which British Railways belatedly recognised some years after the demise of the GWR). Its train services were not either prolific of generally very fast; while many of its less-important lines were a last refuge for aged engines and carriages. Like most branch lines, those of the West Midlands and the Welsh Marches were a fascinating repository of local tradition and life.

Eighty years after it had been absorbed into the GWR and after that mighty giant had itself been swallowed up into British Railways, the old West Midland still survived — albeit only as a Section of the Western Region. Long may it continue to do so!

*Keith M. Beck*
*Taunton*

# 1 The 'Old Worse and Worse' — the Oxford, Worcester & Wolverhampton Railway

There have been a number of railways whose initials lent themselves to alternative — and usually uncomplimentary — names, but few were so well-deserved as the nickname of the 'Old Worse and Worse' given to the Oxford, Worcester & Wolverhampton Railway. For in many ways it *was* one of the worst companies, even at a time when there were quite a few others which could have competed for that title!

Its original aims, conveyed in its title, were without reproach. It was to provide a main line running from Oxford to Wolverhampton by way of Worcester, Kidderminster and Dudley, which would give the city of Worcester its first railway — the only existing line being that of the Midland Railway (formerly Birmingham & Gloucester), whose Spetchley station was situated about three miles to  the east of the city. However, the accomplishing of those simple aims was to involve years of argument, double-dealing and manoeuvres in which the company, the Great Western and, above all, the London & North Western, were to become embroiled. When finally opened, its lack of engines and rolling stock was to produce some of the most hair-raising methods of operation to be encountered anywhere on what was supposed to be a main line, and its grandiose ambitions were almost beyond credulity.

The GWR's branch from Didcot to Oxford was opened in June 1844, and this was followed by the formation of a company, with GWR assistance, to make a broad gauge line from Oxford to Worcester and Wolverhampton, together with sundry short branches. The Act for this line was obtained in the Session of 1845, after a long and hard-fought contest, just at the time what what was known as the 'Battle of the Gauges' was being fought. Shortly afterwards, after another hard fight, the GWR were successful in obtaining powers to extend the broad gauge to Birmingham and Wolverhampton. This meant that the OW&WR had to face the reality of their original dream of becoming *the* broad-gauge route into the West Midlands being destined to be replaced by the GWR lines — as yet unbuilt — and of reducing theirs to secondary importance only.

Added to this, there was a genuine misunderstanding on the part of the shareholders as to the extent to which the GWR would provide financial assistance for the construction of their line; though this may have been due to some deliberately misleading statements made by one or two of their most influential Directors.

The eventual result of all this was the construction of the line with standard-gauge track and a train service provided by courtesy of the LNWR, with Euston rather than Paddington being the station for its London services! The antics and actions of the 'Old Worse and Worse' were to provide one of the final nails for the coffin of the broad gauge, and ensured that standard gauge rails reached Paddington much earlier than might otherwise have been the case.

The OW&WR was intended by its Act to be a line from a junction with the Oxford branch of the GWR (from south of the latter's terminus) to the Wolverhampton station of the Grand Junction Railway at Wednesfield Heath. There were to be branches from Worcester to the Severn at Diglis (which was never built), from Droitwich to the Salt Works at Stoke Prior, and from Brettel Lane to Kingswinsford, while it was to connect with the Birmingham & Gloucester's line at Abbot's Wood, south of Worcester, and at Stoke Prior. Not only was it to be constructed to the satisfaction of the GWR's Engineer — at that time, Brunel — but also 'to be formed of such gauge . . . as will admit of the same being worked continuously with the said Great Western Railway'. In other words, it was to be on the broad gauge; though the section from Abbot's Wood to Wolverhampton was to be of 'mixed' gauges.

The Act also conferred powers to lease or sell the

**1**
Early days on the 'Old Worse and Worse': 2-2-2
No 51 *Will Shakspere* on a Euston to Worcester
train. *LGRP, courtesy David & Charles*

line to the GWR and for the latter Company to
appoint six Directors out of a total number of 16. By
Agreements made in 1844, the GWR guaranteed an
annual payment of £52,000, being 3½% on the
authorised capital of £1,500,000, and half the profits
in return for a 999 year lease of the whole line when
completed. This guarantee was set out prominently in
the prospectus. It was quite natural, in view of such
support, for everyone — not least the GWR — to
assume that the outcome would be the leasing of the
line to the latter Company. Rarely, however, has an
assumption been less grounded in reality.

During the Committee stage, another clause was
inserted in the Act, which was to become of great
importance: this stated that the GWR was willing to
undertake, in case of need, the due completion of the
railway, and empowered that Company, in the event
of the OW&WR neglecting or failing to complete their
line within the agreed period, to proceed to construct it
themselves, and to exercise the powers of the defauling
Company. What was to be of great significance was
the further provision that the GWR were to be *obliged*
to do so if called upon by the Board of Trade.

Almost as soon as the Act was passed it became
apparent that Brunel's original estimate of £1,500,000
had become quite insufficient, due to additional works
being required and rise in the cost of labour and
materials. Francis Rufford, the Chairman, who was a
Stourbridge banker, wrote to the GWR's Chairman

asking that the rent for the lease should be increased
from the fixed sum of £52,000 to 3½% on the
legitimate expenditure found to be necessary. Russell,
the GWR's Chairman, replied that this would not be
acceptable unless there was a definite limit set; and
Brunel, as Engineer, was directed to make revised
estimates for the whole cost of the line. This came to
just under £2,500,000, and the revised estimate was
duly sent to the GWR.

The GWR's Directors decided that the maximum
amount they could guarantee would be £2,500,000
and that the rate of interest could be increased to 4%.
This was confirmed at a general meeting, approval
being given 'for modifying the terms and conditions
previously arranged . . . by extending the guarantee to
*such a sum as shall appear to them* (ie the GWR
Directors) necessary for the completion of the said
railway'. This was to become the root of the bitter
quarrel which was to ensue between the Companies.
The GWR resolution was published by the OW&WR
Directors, but no mention was made of the vital words
which limited the guarantee to £2,500,000. Not only
the OW&WR shareholders, but the general public,
were led to believe that the interest on the whole cost
of the line, *what ever it might be*, was guaranteed by
the GWR.

No formal agreement was made between the Companies — for which the GWR was as much to blame
as the OW&WR — and the GWR did nothing to
refute the statements made by the latter's Directors. It
appears that Rufford, who was said to be an absolute
dictator, was quite confident of getting the GWR to
exceed their limit. However, it was not only agreements which were in an indefinite state: work on the
line itself appeared to be in much the same condition!

In the 1846 Session the OW&WR supported the GWR in respect of an abortive proposal for a broad gauge route to Ireland, which would have been a line from Worcester to Port Dynellin in Caernarvonshire! They also gave support to the Birmingham & Oxford Junction Railway (the 'competing' route to their own line), as they had agreed with the Grand Junction and the GWR. They also obtained an Act for branches to Stratford-on-Avon and Witney. However, in August 1847 the Directors applied to the GWR asking them once again to increase the rate of interest payable under the guarantee, this time to 5%. The latter Company refused to consider this request.

The OW&WR was unable to raise any further money, and the GWR suggested that expenditure should be confined to the line between Oxford and Worcester. When consulted, Brunel agreed that this was the only portion which would produce any profit by which the GWR could pay rent to the owners; authority was reluctantly given to stop work on the northern portion of the line and give priority to the works between Oxford and Worcester. The Company was thus faced with the prospect of their through route linking Paddington with Wolverhampton declining into a branch from Oxford to Worcester!

'All was revealed', as far as the unfortunate shareholders were concerned when Russell was questioned at the GWR's General Meeting about the guarantee and stated explicitly that this was limited to 4% on a sum not exceeding £2,500,000. This caused a sensation and some awkward questions were put, in turn, to the OW&WR's Chairman by some shareholders. They were told that the guarantee was *intended* to cover the whole cost of the line, which was quite literally true yet managed to give a false impression.

The Company was not able to raise further money to complete the whole line, and the Directors asked for authority to make some arrangement with the GWR for payment for rent for a portion of it. They also asked for 'postponement' of interest on the paid-up capital. As events turned out, the unfortunate shareholders were never again to receive any such payment from the Company. Having made to the GWR the required admission concerning the limits of the guarantee, they proposed that the latter Company should lease the section between Oxford and Stourbridge, as soon as finished, at a rent of £84,000. To their chagrin, the GWR declined to do this, suggesting instead that they should work any portion of the line while partially open for the benefit and at the risk of the owners — an arrangement they had agreed with the South Wales Railway. This, in turn, was declined by the OW&WR Directors, and negotiations terminated forthwith.

The latter body was now at a 'dead end'. Nearly all

2

3

the money was spent, none of the railway was ready for opening, and the works were at a standstill. They were compelled to make a complete disclosure of the state of affairs to their shareholders; though the fact were stated clearly enough, there was a quite natural attempt to excuse themselves and place all the blame upon the GWR: they were generally successful in both matters!

The landed gentry then intervened, complaints being made to the Commissioners of Railways by many of the landowners and residents, led by the Duke of Marlborough, of the injury and inconvenience they were suffering by the situation, and calling on them to require the GWR to exercise the power of completing the railway which was given by the Act of 1845. However, the Act contained no provision for raising money to complete the line in such a situation: it only authorised the GWR to exercise the powers of the other Company, which in this respect had been exhausted!

Having been requested to intervene, the Commissioners felt obliged to enforce the provisions of the Act, and directed Captain Simmons to report on the state of the line and to furnish an estimate of the amount of money required to complete it. His report revealed that a great deal of work remained to be done, but the sections from Evesham to Worcester and Stourbridge to near Dudley were 'nearly ready for opening, with the exceptions of the stations and the permanent way not being laid!' This included the

Worcester at the beginning of this century. The Joint station at Shrub Hill, with its overall roof, is to the left of the chimney stack. The engine repair shops are to the rear of the glass-ended carriage shops. The 'wall' between the coaling platform and the through shed was formed by the stack of locomotive coal.
*Author's Collection*

section between Abbot's Wood and Droitwich, with the branch to Stoke Prior, which was obviously of considerable interest to the Midland Railway. A formal order was sent to the GWR in January 1850, requiring them 'forthwith to enter upon the said Railway from Oxford to Worcester and Wolverhampton and to proceed with the construction thereof and to complete the same'. However, the GWR made no attempt to do anything about this.

Representations were also made by the Corporations of Worcester, Kidderminster, Droitwich and Evesham, resulting in a request to the Attorney General to proceed against the GWR. The latter Company stated that the powers of the Act of 1845 were not sufficient to enable them to comply with the order, after which the whole affair dragged through the court for another year.

On 28 April 1851, the Commissioners wrote that 'Having satisfactory grounds for believing that the Railway is in progress towards completion and that it is very probable that it will be opened for public traffic at no very distant period, they no longer consider it necessary to continue the legal proceedings instituted to enforce their order'. This surprising state of affairs was in no way the result of any activity on the part of the GWR, but to unexpected happenings within the OW&WR camp. A Bill had been passed enabling the Company to raise additional capital by means of preference shares.

At long last, on 5 October 1850, the first section of the line, four miles in length, from the junction with the Midland at Abbot's Wood to a temporary station in Worcester, was opened for traffic. It was worked entirely by the MR as a single line branch, and took the place of the omnibus service to and from Spetchley station which for 10 years had been the only connection between the City of Worcester and the railway system of the country.

Messrs Peto and Betts, the well-known contractors, tendered to complete the line from Oxford to Worcester and from Tipton to Wolverhampton within 18 months, while Messrs Treadwells offered to do the same between Worcester and Tipton. The Contractors also offered to find some of the capital required, *provided they were allowed some control in the manage-*

*ment.* Associated with them was John Parson, a London solicitor, who was appointed the Company's legal advisor. He soon established himself in the position of dictator of the Company's policy, resulting in the retirement of the former dictator, Rufford, from the chair. Not long afterwards, Rufford became bankrupt when his bank stopped payment, and the OW&WR lost about £24,000 which it could ill afford. Rufford then disappeared from the affairs of the Company. Though he was largely to blame for the parlous state of the OW&WR's finances, his fellow Directors could not escape censure for some of the events.

Lord Ward of Dudley was persuaded to accept the office of Chairman, but was not destined to enjoy that office for very long. Parson and Peto, with the authority of the Board, opened negotiations with the LNWR and the MR Companies. This resulted in an agreement that the line should be completed as a *standard gauge* one which was to be worked by the two Companies for 24 years. This agreement was sealed by the three Boards on 21 February and adopted by the LNWR's and MR shareholders. However, Lord Ward declined to have anything to do with it, stating that it was beyond the powers of the Company and quite illegal. Parson and the rest of the Board opposed him and the Agreement was adopted. Lord Ward resigned — having first stated that the Board of Directors were a nonentity and the whole of the business was transacted by the Solicitor and the Contractor, who permitted the Board to know only as much as they thought proper!

It was not to be expected that the GWR would sit back and allow the line to fall into the hands of the 'narrow gauge', and steps were taken to show that Lord Ward had been correct and that the Agreement was illegal. Some shareholders of the 'Old Worse and Worse' were not in agreement with what had been done, and obtained an injunction to restrain the Directors from carrying out the Agreement and spending money in laying the standard gauge rails. It was declared that the Agreement effected a lease which the Company had no power to make, and was therefore illegal and void.

The GWR then offered to lease the line on similar terms to those offered by the LNWR and the MR, providing that it was completed throughout as a broad gauge double track, with additional standard gauge rails northwards from Abbot's Wood, as prescribed by the Act. The terms of the lease included the provision of stock by the GWR as well as the working of the line on more favourable terms than those previously agreed with the rival Companies.

The OW&WR Directors, including Parson, strongly recommended the acceptance of these terms. Eventually, after much verbal conflict within the

OW&WR camp, the Agreement was confirmed, subject to a condition that at the end of four years the GWR should buy the line, if called upon to do so, at a price of £30 for each £50 share (the current market price being £14½-15). Parson, who was probably the largest individual shareholder, thought that the GWR would accept this: he was wrong — they refused to be blackmailed!

For the next five years a fight of extreme bitterness raged between the two Companies, giving the little OW&WR the right to be considered a worthy member of the Paddington 'Chamber of Horrors'-hitherto reserved for the permanent occupation of the LSWR with the LNWR and the MR appearing there at regular intervals! The root of the quarrel was the old allegation about the unlimited guarantee, added to which was the refusal of the GWR to lease part of the line when opened. As proceedings to enforce this had been abandoned at the special request of Parson himself, there were little grounds for complaint. However, this did not prevent them being urged on the Parliamentary Committee and the Law Courts during the next five years. The only people to get any satisfaction were the lawyers and the OW&WR shareholders who were being assured of the righteousness of the cause!

The Session of 1852 saw the war begin in earnest, when the OW&WR presented four Bills — one of which was 'dynamite'. This was for an extension line from Wolvercot by Thame, Risborough, Wycombe, Beaconsfield and Uxbridge, *to join the Hounslow branch of the LSWR at Brentford.* The OW&WR had managed to drag in the GWR's most detested enemy! However, this encountered opposition from quite an unexpected quarter, as the LNWR strongly opposed it. It was one thing to discomfort the GWR; it was quite another matter to aid and encourage the LSWR to invade the Midlands by the back door! They also joined in the fight, with a Bill for a junction and branch from their Buckinghamshire line to the OW&WR — and for power to work the latter: this was thrown out by the Lords.

In February 1852 the GWR discovered that the 'Old Worse and Worse' were proceeding with the layout of the standard gauge rails, but not those for the broad gauge; and that this was being done between Abbot's Wood and Evesham, where they were not authorised. The GWR therefore sought to restrain the OW&WR from laying standard-gauge rails south of Abbot's Wood, and from laying them north of that point until they had completed the broad gauge throughout.

Parson's response was an affidavit that they intended to construct the *whole line* on the mixed gauge and that it was to be double between Wolverhampton and Norton Junction or perhaps Evesham, and single for the remainder, to be doubled when funds permitted. He specifically denied that they intended any portion of the line to be permanently worked on the standard gauge only. This was coupled with a statement — though not the reasons for it — that the Company's funds were sufficient to complete the whole line on the mixed gauge!

A further section, from Worcester through Droitwich to the junction with the MR at Stoke Works, nearly nine and three-quarters miles, was opened on 18 February 1852, as a double standard gauge line, with room for the addition of broad gauge rails. This meant that there was now a complete loop through Worcester from the MR's Birmingham & Gloucester main line, the whole being worked entirely by the latter Company. At this stage, the OW&WR possessed neither engines nor rolling stock.

On 1 May 1852 the sections of the main line

**4**
Charlbury station, typical of the country stations on the OW&WR main line. 1932.
*LGRP, courtesy David & Charles*

between Droitwich and Stourbridge and Norton and Evesham were opened, making with the existing 'loop' a stretch of 36 miles. A contract was made with 'Mr Williams, the carriage builder of Goswell Street, for the supply of the necessary locomotives and carrying stock'. At first there were one or two short sections of single track, but by the end of July the whole line was finished as a standard gauge double line 'with the requisite provisions for carrying out the Act of Parliament for the broad gauge'. A further section of six miles, from Stourbridge to Dudley, was opened on 20 December.

When Russell, the GWR's Chairman, offered new terms for a lease or to provide engine power on fair terms (though the GWR had no standard gauge engines and the OW&WR possessed no broad gauge track!), the reply was that a fresh application was to be made for the Oxford and Brentford scheme and that, as the Directors 'cannot see the possibility of reconciling therewith an amicable working of their line by the Great Western, they decline to attempt it'. The Brentford project was revived as the London & Mid Western, with a branch to Aylesbury and a short spur to the LNWR at Willesden; while another line was alsp proposed to link Cheltenham and Oxford, under the title of the Cheltenham & Oxford Union Railway. Once again, the capital was subscribed by Parson and the Contractors, there being little local support.

The GWR's response was to apply for an injunction to restrain the Company from opening their line from Evesham to Wolvercot until the whole line was provided with the broad gauge. Parson soon produced another affidavit that the Directors still intended to complete the whole line on the mixed gauge 'so as to admit of the same being worked continuously with the Great Western' and that there were now ample funds available.

The battle ended with the GWR consenting that 'every facility should be given to the traffic of the Oxford, Worcester & Wolverhampton Railway, whether on the broad or narrow gauge, and that suitable arrangements should be made to admit their trains to and from the Great Western station at Oxford, so that the public may have no impediment in the change of trains. As the Oxford & Rugby line was mixed gauge, there was no problem.

After several delays due to the unsatisfactory condition of some of the track — the outer rails for the broad gauge only being hand-packed and unable to bear the weight of an engine! — the Inspector eventually travelled to Evesham and back with his broad gauge engine and carriage on 2 June, and sanctioned the opening of the mixed gauge single line. At long last, the line was opened on Saturday 4 June 1853, though special advance celebrations had taken place on 7 May — the day concluding with the usual sumptuous dinner at which hopes of the success of the Mid Western project were to be heard. By the actual opening day, both the Mid Western and the Cheltenham & Oxford schemes had been rejected by the Commons Committee!

However, the LNWR had been successful with their Bill for a branch, one and a half miles long, to join the OW&WR at Yarnton, and this was destined to provide that Company with its desired standard gauge outlet to the south. Until this line was opened, the OW&WR's goods service south of Evesham consisted of one train each night from Dudley to Handborough and back. Five passenger trains on weekdays and two on Sundays were run to and from Oxford throughout the summer of 1853. At this time, the broad gauge rail was added to the Down line throughout between

**5**

Campden station c1910. A 'Standard Goods' 0-6-0 is engaged in shunting. There were evidently cheap fares to London on Mondays, though how many local people contemplated travelling by the Cunard Line is doubtful! *H. G. W. Household collection*

Evesham and Dudley; but no broad gauge sidings or crossing places were provided and the up line remained exclusively standard gauge. This was the Company's limits in pretending to be carrying out their obligations.

Another obligation was the doubling of the 40 miles of line between Evesham and Wolvercot, though this was also needed for traffic purposes. By November the sections between Evesham and Honeybourne, and Handborough and Wolvercot, had been doubled, and the Board of Trade was invited to inspect them. As the latter section was complete as a double mixed gauge line, it was passed for opening. However, the new up line between Evesham and Honeybourne was laid on the standard gauge only, and the Inspector reported that it was not safe for a mixed gauge line to be worked as a double line on one gauge and as a single line on the other. Therefore, the Board of Trade 'directed the Company to postpone such opening for the period of one calendar month'.

The scene was now set for something which was to approach a West End farce. The Company took no notice of the order and opened the line, their Secretary meanwhile writing letters to the Board protesting that they had no intention of working any portion of the line on the broad gauge! He also undertook that the Company would submit the line for further inspection before allowing broad gauge working: however, the broad gauge rail would be laid *when additional capital had been raised*. The latter statement came not long after Parson's affidavits that there was plenty of money for that purpose!

Shortly after the line was opened, the Traffic Manager, W. T. Adcock, submitted his proposals to the Board of Trade for their necessary approval of the 'cheap train' arrangements — and this proved to be the 'undoing' of the 'Old Worse and Worse'. Some one noticed that an up train was so timed that it passed a down train between Evesham and Honeybourne, which was still a single line according to the Board of Trade. They therefore wrote to request an explanation of how this was done, as only one line was officially open! The reply was, 'Passenger trains on the narrow gauge are now daily running on the up line between Evesham and Honeybourne, the Directors being advised that Captain Galton's refusal to sanction the opening for the reasons he gave was not within his functions'. The only source of such advice must have been Parson himself.

The response of the Board was to get the Attorney General to obtain an injunction restraining the Company from using the up line between Evesham and Honeybourne for passenger trains until it had been sanctioned by the Board of Trade. As a result the up line was closed for traffic on 18 March 1854, and single line working from Evesham to Handborough

was resumed. There followed a monthly inspection of the line, with a monthly report which was always the same. This was followed by a copy being sent each month with a letter from the Board of Trade to the Company directing them 'to postpone the opening of the second line of rails referred to, for the public conveyance of passengers, for a further period of one calendar month from this date'. At first these provoked a flood of letters, affidavits, interviews, copies of Minutes; anything, in fact, except compliance with the law!

However, none of these made any impression, as the Board insisted that the law must be obeyed — and they won! By the end of the year the Company had been worn down by this unyielding stand, and on his January visit the Captain found that steps were actually being taken to add the third rail. In March he was even able to report that the mixed gauge was complete on the up line from Evesham as far as Campden, and that the line was to be worked by telegraph. The Board sanctioned the opening on 20 March 1853, almost exactly a year after it had been closed.

Meanwhile, the line between Charlbury and Handborough had been doubled on the mixed gauge, duly sanctioned, and opened on 1 August 1854. The intervening 20 miles between Charlbury and Campden remained single track until August 1858, by which time the fight over the gauge had been concluded.

Long before this, war with the GWR had been resumed in the autumn of 1853. The latter Company applied for a declaration that the OW&WR should be constructed with a double line of rails on the broad gauge throughout its entire length and should not be allowed to construct any additional lines on the standard gauge until this was done, and the Board of Trade was also asked to take measures to enforce the law. That body had also received complaints from several titled persons and influential landowners complaining of the inconvenience of the break of gauge at Oxford, of the refusal of the Company to work the broad gauge or allow it to be worked, and of the proposal to send London passengers round by Bletchley instead of by the 10 miles shorter GWR route. Some of them must have suffered from claustrophobia, as among the complaints was that the LNWR line involved passing through several tunnels, while there were none on the GWR's route!

An injunction was granted, despite the production of the usual affidavits by the OW&WR, and the Company was stopped from spending more and more money on standard gauge works until they had completed the double line of broad gauge over the whole of their system.

While all this was taking place, further portions of the railway were opened. The line from Dudley to the junction and the Stour Valley Railway at Tipton was

**6**
Kingham station, showing the branch platforms. The Banbury line curves away to the right, where an auto train stands in front of the engine shed. Trains for Cheltenham had to cross the main line which passed under the girder bridge in the distance carrying the Banbury & Cheltenham Direct Line.
*LGRP, courtesy David & Charles*

brought into use on 1 December 1853, as a double standard gauge line with a broad gauge rail on part of the line only! On 1 April 1854, the LNWR's branch to Yarnton was opened. A traffic agreement had already been made, which provided that all traffic to and from London, and from places south and east of Oxford, should travel via Bletchley, the distance between Euston and Yarnton being taken as 65 miles instead of the actual 76 miles. In return, the LNWR were to have the whole traffic between London and Wolverhampton, also half of that from Dudley. This agreement was to last for 21 years, but as it had no Parliamentary authority — being one of Captain Huish's notorious agreements, for which the LNWR's General Manager was well-known — it was not legally enforceable.

The through service between Euston and Worcester, with trains continuing via Tipton to the High Level station at Wolverhampton, commenced at once. Connecting trains were run by the GWR between their Oxford station and that station at 'Handborough Junction', as there was no station at Yarnton until the Witney branch was opened in 1861, so that it was still possible to travel to and from Paddington, though this meant re-booking at Oxford. The fastest time between London and Worcester by the Bletchley route was 4 hours, this being by one train in each direction. For many years after the transfer of through passenger services to Paddington, the title 'Handborough Junction' was retained both in the Time Tables and on the station's notice boards!

The main line from Tipton to a temporary station at Wolverhampton and on to Cannock Road Junction was opened on 1 July 1854. This was a double line of mixed gauge, as GWR trains were to use it from Priestfield Junction — the first one doing so in November. The remaining mile to the LNWR at Bushbury was opened as a standard gauge line in July, for goods traffic only — though it was authorised for passenger trains in October. Apart from a very short-lived service between Wolverhampton (Low Level) and Manchester in 1864-6 (which ceased as soon as the opening of the Wellington to Nantwich line allowed the GWR access to Crewe), it was never used for passenger traffic except for the regular passage of the Royal Train during the years of Queen Victoria and by Ambulance Trains during the war years.

This completed the OW&WR main line, much of which was still not provided with broad gauge double track: there was only one broad gauge siding on the entire line, this being at Bilston — and the reason for its existence remains a mystery! The only broad gauge train to run over any part of the line south of Priestfield Junction was Captain Galton's inspection train from Wolvercot to Evesham and back on 2 June 1853. It is most unlikely that any of the broad gauge track north of Evesham was ever in a fit state to carry an engine, let alone a train.

By this time the Company was on the verge of ruin: the receipts were hardly sufficient to pay the dividend on the 6% preference shares; the rolling stock was inadequate for the traffic; and the second-hand engines provided for the line for the contractor were more often broken down than in use — these forming one of the most weird collections ever assembled at one place.

In every way, the line thoroughly deserved its nickname of the 'Old Worse and Worse'.

Despite this, there was yet another attempt to get Parliament to release the Company from the broad gauge and all powers of the GWR. This was again defeated in 1855. Parliament consistently refused to release the Company from its obligations to lay the broad gauge, yet it would neither compel them to work it when laid nor grant the GWR power to do so! The Directors were now left with no alternative but to complete the broad gauge double line, though they publicly stated that it would be a waste of time and money — having ensured by their conduct that this would be the case!

At this time the Company again came to the attention of the Board of Trade, this time by reason of the state of its rolling stock. There had been a delay of six hours near Hartlebury to the evening down 'Express' train on 18 October 1855, which was caused by the successive failures of four engines. These were the regular engine for the train, the engine which took it on from Worcester, and two sent one after the other to its rescue!

The Company managed to obtain further Acts which gave them four years in which to complete the broad gauge. The position began to improve, with the working expenses reduced from 68%, to 51% during consecutive half years. The locomotive stock had also been greatly improved. The permanent way, which consisted of bridge rails on longitudinal timbers, like that of the GWR appears to have been reasonably maintained from the beginning. The Company was now able to work all its own traffic, and the LNWR was no longer required to work the traffic south of Handborough and from Dudley to Wolverhampton.

After many conferences and much correspondence, the disputes with the GWR were finally settled and an Agreement was signed in February 1858. The GWR agreed to the broad gauge being removed south of Priestfield Junction, and received £2,000 per annum for nine years in 'compensation' for the absence of agreement that a defined amount of traffic should be sent over the GWR (due to the existing agreement with the LNWR and MR). The OW&WR were to run at least three passenger trains daily over their line in connection with GWR trains at Oxford. Most important, neither Company should promote or assist in any way any new line competing with the other. This last clause was to be the cause of a considerable amount of recrimination within a short time.

The broad gauge rails remained — though not all of them: some had already been taken up and sold either to the GWR(!) or to the Worcester & Hereford Railway. Those that did remain were to be seen for many years, as a rusty memorial to the fierce and bitter struggles of the past — and of John Parson's triumph not only over the GWR, but also the Court of Chancery and even Parliament itself!

The only event to shatter the tranquility of the remaining days of the Company's existence was what Captain Tyler of the Board of Trade described as 'Decidedly the worst railway accident that has ever occurred in this country'. This was on 2 August 1858, when a packed excursion train returning from Worcester to Wolverhampton broke into two sections, the rear 17 carriages running back down a 1 in 75 bank to collide with a second excursion train just leaving Brettell Lane. Fourteen people were killed and 50 seriously injured.

Having cut right through the Moreton-in-Marsh terminus of the existing Stratford & Moreton Railway, an ancient horse tramway, the Company agreed in 1844 to take a perpetual lease of it. In 1855 the single line branch to Chipping Norton was opened 'from a junction with the main line situated midway between Shipton and Addlestrop stations, where a house has been erected for the issue of tickets to passengers'. The line, which was opened on 10 August was constructed as a local undertaking, though worked by the OW&WR who purchased it in 1859. The house at the junction later became Chipping Norton Junction station, renamed Kingham in 1909.

The MR already provided a 'second presence' in Worcester, at the joint station at Shrub Hill, and in 1860 a third line made its appearance. This was the Worcester & Hereford, incorporated as early as 1853, but unable to raise sufficient capital to begin its work. The 'Old Worse and Worse', having assumed a more respectable image, was persuaded by the Newport, Abergavenny & Hereford Railway to join in subscribing towards the building of the line to connect the two cathedral cities. This actually brought about the end of the OW&WR as an independent Company, for the friendly relations established with the NA&HR led to proposals for amalgamation and joint purchase of the connecting W.&MR line. A Bill to amalgamate the three Companies as the West Midland Railway was passed in 1860.

Special facilities were given to the traffic of the MR, who had subscribed largely to the W&MR, from Worcester to South Wales. Another 'Hereford' Company, the Shrewsbury & Hereford, obtained running powers over the line of the former NA&HR in exchange for similar powers of their line being granted to the new WMR. Both these were to assume considerable importance, in ways not imagined — and certainly not intended — at a later date. They were to be the doors by which both the MR and the LNWR entered South Wales, and were to result in these Companies (and later the LMS) having enclaves in what might well have been considered to be a GWR preserve.

# 2 'Rails to Hereford'

## Shrewsbury & Hereford Railway

Hereford's first rail connection with the rest of the country was not, as might have been expected, with Gloucester where the broad gauge had been firmly established since May 1845, nor with that other member of the Three Choirs Festival, Worcester, but with the county town of Shropshire.

The Shrewsbury & Hereford Railway was sanctioned by Parliament in 1846, in preference to a broad gauge line from the proposed Monmouth & Hereford Railway. The engineer for the $50\frac{1}{2}$ miles of standard gauge line was Henry Robertson. Owing to the general financial troubles of the time, no serious beginning was made until the end of 1850, when the famous Thomas Brassey took a contract to make the line and offered to work it at his own risk, paying $3\frac{1}{2}\%$ on the cost. His offer was accepted and afterwards changed into a lease for nine years from 1 July 1853, during the last four years of which he was able to pay the Company 4% and half surplus profits: a very different situation from that on the 'Old Worse and Worse'!

The railway was opened as a single line from Shrewsbury to Ludlow, a distance of $27\frac{1}{2}$ miles, on 20 April 1852, with the final section to Hereford opening on 6 December 1853. At Shrewsbury the Company shared in the use of the Joint Station with three other lines, the Shrewsbury & Chester, the Shrewsbury & Birmingham, and the Shropshire Union (later to be absorbed by the LNWR). At Hereford the terminus was at Barr's Court, on the eastern side of the city. Initially the first section as far as Ludlow was worked by the Shrewsbury & Chester.

The S&HR's workshops and engine sheds were at Coleham, Shrewsbury — later considerably enlarged and developed under the joint ownership of the SWR and LNWR. At Hereford there was an engine shed at the north end of Barr's Court station, while a small shed was opened in 1853 at Leominster and another at Ludlow in about 1857. After the S&HR was taken over jointly be the GWR and LNWR the shed at Hereford was used exclusively by the LNWR while that at Leominster became the property of the GWR. The Hereford shed was closed in 1935.

There were no branches until 1857, when the independent Leominster & Kington Railway was opened — using the S&HR's shed at Leominster to stable its two small tank engines. The five miles of the independent Tenbury Railway from Woofferton were opened in 1861, and an engine shed for its one locomotive was provided at Woofferton; this shed was closed in 1896.

The Company led a fairly peaceful life and was quite prosperous, so that Brassey was handing over sufficient money in 1860 for a dividend of 6% to be paid on its ordinary shares. It enjoyed good relations with its southern neighbour, the NA&HR, whose station at Hereford was on the other side of the city, at Barton, though there was a connecting line. The S&HR had opposed the formation of the WMR and as a result had obtained running powers over the whole of the former NA&HR line in return for similar powers being given to the WMR between Hereford and Shrewsbury for traffic to and from Newport.

The unlikely news of the GWR and WMR Agreement fell like a bombshell into the untroubled world of the Company's Directors. The GWR was established at both ends of their line (having absorbed the S&CR and the S&BR, as well as having opened a broad gauge line from Gloucester to Hereford), and the WMR was about to open the Severn Valley line into Shrewsbury as well as the Worcester & Hereford Railway; both of the latter could be used to divert traffic from the S&HR. Brassey's lease had little more than a year to run, after which they would have to purchase rolling stock and fend for themselves, with no guarantee of a 6% dividend! They at once approached the LNWR, who lost no time in offering to take a perpetual lease of the line on terms which would guarantee the magic 6% to the ordinary shareholders. However, the LNWR proposed — most uncharacteristically for that Company — that it would be politic to invite the GWR to join with them in the lease.

Far from responding with alacrity, as might have been expected, the GWR intimated that they would contest the proposals. Now the LNWR already possessed running powers, acquired by agreement, over the S&HR but were not entitled to proceed south of Hereford. What neither the GWR nor the WMR were prepared to contemplate was the prospect of the LNWR taking over the running powers of the S&HR and thus being able to gain access to the coalfields of South Wales — especially as they had recently succeeded in acquiring the Merthyr, Tredegar & Abergavenny Railway, just as the newly-formed WMR had thought it was going to do so!

However, the Euston interest and determination were not going to be deterred by such declared opposition, and the result was the joint promotion by the S&HR and the LNWR of a Bill in the Session of 1862 to authorise the lease to the latter Company alone, but reserving power to admit the GWR to share it on terms to be agreed. Despite this, both the GWR and

the WMR continued to fight fiercely against the Bill, but without success; the Commons Committee would not even cancel the running powers which were the cause of all the trouble. They were forced to make the best of a bad job, withdraw their opposition, and agree to share equally with the LNWR in the lease.

As from 1 July 1862, the S&HR became the joint property of the three Companies, the LNWR having a half share. Mr Brassey's stock was then purchased by the S&HR and divided between the new owners. Arrangements were made for doubling the line throughout, except for Dinmore Tunnel (1,056yd) which was not done until 1893. The northern section between Shrewsbury and Ludlow had already been doubled.

**The Newport, Abergavenny & Hereford Railway**
The Newport, Abergavenny & Hereford's origins were to be found in one of the many grandiose schemes of the 'Railway Mania' of 1844-6 which failed to materialise. This was for the 'Welsh Midland Railway', which was intended to be a line running from the Birmingham & Gloucester near Worcester, through Hereford and Brecon to Merthyr, where it was to connect with the Taff Vale Railway — by means of which it would reach Cardiff — and on to Swansea. The NA&HR was conceived as a local line to connect the Welsh Midland with Newport. Enough local support was obtained to make it possible to obtain a Bill in 1846, which received the Royal Assent on the same day as that for the S&HR.

However, despite its title, the Act did not authorise the railway to make a line to Newport, but only as far as Pontypool; the Monmouthshire Railway & Canal

**7**

Foregate Street station bridge, with the heraldic shields newly repainted for the Coronation in 1953. No 6989 *Wightwick Hall* is on a Paddington to Hereford train. *R. J. Doran*

**8**
'717' class 2-4-0 No 722 stands in Great Malvern station on a Birmingham to Cardiff train in 1894. Half a dozen engines of this little-known class were for many years the only passenger tender engine shedded at the old Bordesley Junction shed.
*LGRP, courtesy David & Charles*

Company having already been empowered to make a line from that place to Newport. There were already three tramways in existence between Abergavenny and Hereford — though all called themselves Railway Companies — which the new Company was empowered, and indeed obliged, to buy out. Two more Acts were passed in 1847, one of which was of considerable significance as it authorised the Taff Vale Extension from the main line in Llanvrechva to a junction with the Taff Vale Railway near Quaker's Yard. This was to provide an immense amount of coal traffic for the Company and its successors, and eventually became part of a through line linking Pontypool with Neath.

The Company had by this time purchased the three tramways, though only the deposits had been paid. A contact for the main line between Pontypool and Abergavenny was let to Messrs Rennie & Logan of Newport, but this was suspended by the end of the year owing to financial troubles. An extension of time both for the purchase of land and for the completion of the railways was granted by the Railway Commissioners. The unfortunate owners of the three tramways were obliged to agree to the postponement of the full purchase price. After this the Company did nothing for three years — and did it well! To quote a classic description, it 'sank into a sleep destined to last for three years, disturbed only by half-yearly meetings

in London, at which the Directors administered a further sleeping draught to such few Proprietors who were wakeful enough to attend' (McDermott).

In 1851 there came a startling announcement that 'influential parties' were taking an interest in the Company and that there were prospects of action being taken. The 'influential parties' were, in fact, none other than the LNWR who were looking for ways of 'invading' South Wales. The Directors announced that they had engaged Mr Charles Liddell as Engineer, and were taking steps to purchase the land for the main line. They were now quite confident that the S&HR was certain to be made, giving a direct line to Birkenhead, while a line from Worcester to Hereford was being promoted jointly by the LNWR and MR. By March 1852 the works were in active progress and the Board had concluded a working agreement with the LNWR to come into force with the opening of the ostensibly independent Worcester & Hereford Railway. However, the latter was not passed by the Lords, and the LNWR then proposed to absorb the NA&HR as well as making a fresh application for the W&HR the following year. The Newport Company then sought authority to sell or lease their line to the LNWR and to extend it to Swansea and Brecon. Alas for the LNWR's plans, it was just at this time that the Cardwell Committee reported very firmly against railway amalgamation in general.

Work on the main line proceeded well, and the purchase of the three tramways was finally completed — no doubt to the great relief of their owners! As the tram-plates were sold soon afterwards at only 15s a ton less than the cost of new iron rails and the remaining property was sold at auction, the Company did quite well out of their purchases. Early in 1853 land was bought for the Taff Vale extension, and by the autumn work had begun on two major engineering works, the tunnel at Hafodyrhys and the great viaduct at Crumlin which was stated to be the largest in the world. The viaduct was to cross the Ebbw Valley at a maximum height of 200ft and to be no less than 1,650ft long, with two sections divided at the top by an intervening hill — the longer section being 1,066ft.

On 6 December, the formal opening of both the S&HR and the NA&HR was celebrated with the usual great demonstrations. However, these were a little premature in the latter case, as owing to an extensive slip in the deep cutting at Llanvihangel, the Board of Trade Inspector, Captain Wynne, ordered a postponement of the opening — which was perhaps just as well, as the station buildings were far from complete! The actual opening for traffic of the double line of Barlow rails from Coedygric Junction, a mile south of Pontypool, to the Barton station in Hereford took place on 2 January 1854. There were no engineering works of any magnitude, which was fortunate for the Company who were faced with the gigantic task of building the Crumlin Viaduct.

Barton station was quite separate from the S&HR's station at Barr's Court, but was connected with the latter line by a mile long loop which allowed for through running between Newport and Shrewsbury, but not between the two stations. This mile of track was actually part of the W&HR who intended using Barton station, and was made on their behalf by the NA&HR at the cost of the other Company (who never paid for it!). While of little use to the NA&HR for passenger traffic, it had tremendous potential as the means by which coal from the Monmouthshire collieries could be transported north to Birkenhead — and it was the latter traffic which was to be the life blood of the Company.

At the other end of the line, arrangements had been made with the Monmouthshire Railway for trains to work through to Newport, where passengers used the latter's Mill Street station. However, no running powers were granted to the Company.

The traffic was worked from the opening by the LNWR, under a temporary agreement pending the completion of the W&HR — an event which did not take place for another seven years! No doubt, the LNWR had hopes of this arrangement becoming a permanent one and eventually leading to their swallowing up the small Company; and thus making the matter of their obtaining a foothold in Monmouthshire a fairly easy process. However, this arrangement did not last for very long, as the Company found themselves being penalised by the LNWR's determination to crush the S&BR and the S&CR, both of whom had had the temerity to make traffic arrangements with the GWR — and the broad gauge — and not, as all good standard gauge lines were expected to do, with the LNWR! Captain Huish, the LNWR's General Manager — one of the arch-villains of the

railway world, not least in GWR eyes — refused to quote through rates between Pontypool and either Birkenhead or Wolverhampton by the direct routes involving the two Shrewsbury lines, insisting that all traffic be sent from Shrewsbury over the LNWR's line by way of Stafford!

The NA&HR refused to be used in this way, and put an end to the working agreement; this was terminated by mutual consent on 1 October. They also abandoned a renewed application to sell their line to the LNWR. As Huish's actions resulted in Parliament agreeing to the amalgamation of the two offending Shrewsbury Companies with the GWR, as well as the LNWR losing their temporary toehold in Monmouthshire, on this occasion that gentleman had been 'too clever by half'.

The Company asked Brassey, the lessee of the S&HR, to provide locomotives, while they would take the working of the traffic into their own hands. As they possessed no rolling stock of any kind, this obviously presented them with some difficulties! However, the LNWR kindly took pity and agreed to continue to provide carriages and other rolling stock: no doubt hoping to retrieve something out of the collapse of all their plans. As Brassey could only spare a limited number of engines, the amount of traffic was reduced: the Company therefore decided to take over the full working of their line. They commenced doing this on 1 January 1855, with four goods and three passenger engines — hardly sufficient for the length of line and amount of traffic. The LNWR added to their difficulties when they withdrew all their rolling stock at the end of March, and as the contractor had failed to deliver the new carriages and wagons which had been promised for 1 March the Company was in great difficulties and lost a large amount of traffic. The S&CR came to their rescue in the matter of engines, lending them several — that Company always appearing to have far more than they needed!

Work had been proceeding on the Taff Vale Extension, and the first section between Pontypool Road and the east side of the valley at Crumlin was opened on 20 August 1855. At first this was a single line laid with Barlow rails, and was to be worked by one engine, but the line was doubled soon afterwards. The branch to the Monmouthshire's Western Valleys line at Llanhilleth was completed at the same time. The Crumlin Viaduct was finished in May 1857, and after being thoroughly tested with heavy loads by the Board of Trade Inspector was opened for traffic on 1 June, as were a further three miles of single line to Pontllanfraith (originally Tredegar Junction). The extension was completed on 11 January 1858, when the remaining section to a junction with the TVR at Quaker's Yard (Low Level) was opened. Although powers had been obtained for a further extension to join the

9

10

**9**

Nearly 60 years later, Great Malvern station —
although shorn of its clock tower and fleche — still
retains much of its ornate scroll work.   *R. J. Doran*

**10**

Pontrilas station in 1932. A typical ex-NA&HR
country station, Pontrilas was the junction for the
Golden Valley line which can be seen leaving the main
line just beyond the signal box.
*LGRP, courtesy David & Charles*

**11**

No 6355 leaving the south end of Hereford, Barr's
Court, on a freight train for Gloucester, May 1949.
*K. W. Wightman/Ian Allan Library*

11

12

13

22

Dinmore Tunnel between Hereford and Leominster on the S&HR. Originally a single bore, a second tunnel was excavated for the up line in 1893. *Real Photos*


The important junction station at Leominster was dominated by the signalbox high above the down platform. Branch trains from New Radnor and Worcester via Bromyard used the far lines. *R. C. Riley*

Aberdare branch of the Vale of Neath Railway (a broad gauge line), this did not take place during the lifetime of the Company.

In 1853 the Coleford, Monmouth, Usk & Pontypool Railway Company was formed to make the line described by its title — though there were one or two additional stations not mentioned in it, and it never reached Coleford! Running from a junction with the NA&HR at Little Mill, about two miles north of Pontypool Road, the first section of the line as far as Usk was opened on 2 June 1856, this being worked by the NA&HR. The line was extended as far as Monmouth (Troy) on 12 October 1857, after which the owners worked it for themselves; though they hired a couple of engines from the NA&HR in order to do this.

Throughout its independent existence, the NA&HR was dependent on the S&HR for its connection with the rest of the railway system. Both the Monmouthshire and the TVR, with which it connected, were only local lines, and the GWR at both Hereford and Newport was of a different gauge! The failure of successive plans to connect Worcester with Hereford were therefore of considerable concern to the Company, and in 1857 they took steps with the aid of the now reformed OW&WR (and later with the MR) to provide financial support for the W&HR so that it was at last commenced in the following year. This action proved to be the means by which the NA&HR ceased to be an independent railway, as it led to the formation of the West Midland Railway on 1 July 1860.

The main offices of the Company were at Barton station and were of interest in being attached to the engine shed and repair shops! In addition to this shed, the Company opened a small shed at Abergavenny, for banking engines, in January 1854. How they managed, as far as shed facilities were concerned, at Pontypool is not at all certain; though some provision must have been made. The GWR's Pontypool Road shed dated from the late 1860s; however, there may have been some earlier premises as something would

have been needed for the engines working on the Taff Vale extension line. Engines on 'main line' trains to Newport would have used the Newport shed of the Monmouthshire Railway.

**The Worcester & Hereford Railway**
The genesis of the Worcester & Hereford Railway went back to 1846, with rival schemes on the broad and narrow (standard) gauges being projected. The Welsh Midland, previously mentioned, was backed by the MR; its rival, a broad gauge line laid out under Brunel's direction, to connect the OW&WR with the proposed Monmouth & Hereford Railway, was needless to say backed by the GWR. However, both schemes were abandoned in the following year and it was not until 1851 that anything further was done. The LNWR then took the matter up, as one of their many steps in the invasion of South Wales: such a line would link their ally, the MR, with the NA&HR which the LNWR had every intention — and considerable hopes — of annexing for themselves.

Charles Liddell, the Engineer of the NA&HR, accordingly laid out a line from the south end of the Shrub Hill station of the OW&WR to cross the Severn and the Teme south of Worcester; by this, both Malvern and Ledbury were to be served by branches, which pleased neither of those towns. It was promoted in the Session of 1852 ostensibly by an independent Company, but in reality by a consortium of the LNWR, the MR and the NA&HR. Both the GWR and the S&HR opposed this project which was eventually rejected by the Lords, whereupon the promoters announced their intention of making a fresh application during the following year.

Both sides prepared for what was expected to be a bitter fight. Amazing to relate, the GWR and the OW&WR joined forces to promote an alternative scheme, the Worcester & Hereford Junction Railway, laid out by Brunel and Fowler. This was to be a mixed gauge line from the south of Shrub Hill station, crossing the Severn by an opening bridge at Diglis Lock, and passing through Great Malvern to join the authorised broad gauge Hereford, Ross & Gloucester line as well as the two existing standard gauge lines at Hereford; there was to be a three mile long branch to Ledbury.

Liddell's rival line was totally different from that of the previous year. In order to obtain support from the Corporation at Worcester, it was now to leave from the north end of Shrub Hill, provide a central station in Foregate Street, and cross the river by a fixed bridge. It was also to pass through Malvern Link and Great Malvern, and within a mile of Ledbury — thus making a bid for local support — to join the S&HR at Shelwick Junction, two miles north of Hereford. Involved in this was the purchase of considerable numbers of houses in Worcester and the boring of two long tunnels; thus the estimated cost of the line was greatly increased.

The mixed gauge proposal was defeated and the W&HR emerged as the victor. The defeated 'partners' were unable to secure the addition of broad-gauge rails to the successful scheme, which was probably just as well when the consistent refusal of the OW&WR to provide such rails on its own line is taken into account. However, the victors were not allowed to have all their own way, as the Lord's insisted that it must be a genuine independent Company and struck out all the clauses which gave powers of subscription or working to the LNWR and MR. As most of the 'subscribers' were dependents of the LNWR the Lord's action quite devastated them! Nothing was done either to raise capital or to proceed with the works, the excuse offered being the general state of the economy.

The NA&HR had withdrawn in disgust from the consortium in 1854; but eight representatives now came back to form a majority on the Board, and negotiations were opened with the OW&WR. This resulted in an agreement to provide capital and work the line when it should be completed. Work on the line was soon begun in earnest on the section from Worcester to Malvern, which was double track: this

included a short northward loop line at Worcester to provide for through running to and from Wolverhampton to the new Foregate Street station and on to Hereford. From Malvern to Shelwick Junction, on the S&HR line, the line was single track. At Shelwick Junction, a connecting line towards Shrewsbury had been authorised, but this was never built.

The first section to be opened was the six miles from Henwick, on the West bank of the Severn, to Malvern Link, which came into use on 25 July 1859, and this was worked by the OW&WR (an engine and stock being transported to Henwick by road). The line from Shrub Hill to Henwick included a long viaduct through the city, on part of which Foregate Street station was built. The iron bridge over the Severn was completed towards the end of the year, but two of the spans required stiffening before the Inspector would allow passenger trains to use the bridge. The line from Shrub Hill to Henwick was opened on 17 May 1860, and a week later the line was extended from Malvern Link through Great Malvern to Malvern Wells, a distance of two miles.

The completion of the remaining 20 miles to Shelwick Junction depended on the excavation of the two long tunnels at Malvern and Ledbury. Before this section was opened, on 17 September 1861, the

14

W&WR had ceased to exist as such, and it was as part of the WMR that the line was opened throughout between the two cities.

## The Hereford, Ross & Gloucester Railway

The imposing title hid the fact that this was a rather typical GWR broad-gauge branch line. It was opened from Grange Court as far as Hopebrook, just over five miles, on 11 July 1853, the remaining $17\frac{1}{2}$ miles not being completed until nearly two years later, being opened on 1 June 1855. It was a single line and unusual in having Barlow rails, and not the usual broad gauge bridge rail on longitudinal timbers which even the OW&WR had used — albeit for the most part on the standard-gauge.

At Hereford the station at Barr's Court was a joint one, shared with the S&HR, despite the difference in gauge. At the time the line opened, the station was far from complete — even though the S&HR had been using it for 18 months. The purely broad gauge track extended through the station on the west side, most of that on the east side being mixed. There was a two-road broad gauge engine shed for the GWR at the south end of the station, on the east side, with a two-road carriage shed on the opposite side of the line. However, the broad gauge goods shed was situated at

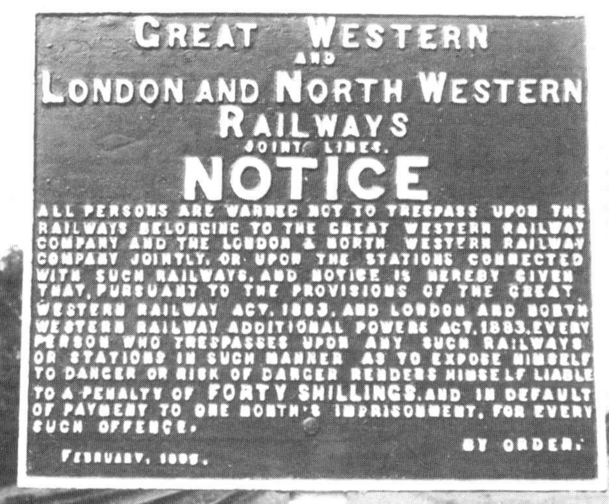

**14**
Leominster station looking south in 1951. No 1455 had just arrived on a branch train from Kington. *R. C. Riley*

**15, 16**
GWR and LNWR Joint notice boards could still be seen at Ashford Bowdler in 1951. *C. R. L. Coles*

A vital service rarely recognised was that of the Crossing Keeper. Mr Jones winds open the crossing gates at Ashford Bowdler in 1951.   *C. R. L .Coles*

17 the north end of the stations, opposite the S&HR's goods premises. Following the conversion of the HR&G line to standard gauge in 1869, the GWR engine shed was closed (being used for many years as a carriage shed) and all engines used the former NA&HR shed at Barton.

## The Hereford, Hay & Brecon Railway

The Hereford, Hay & Brecon Railway was opened between the places named on its title in September 1864, though its actual line only reached as far as Three Cocks Junction; access to Brecon being over the tracks of the Mid Wales Railway (later Cambrian Railways) to Talyllyn Junction, and thence over those of the Brecon & Merthyr Railway. Although never part of the GWR, two of its stations — at Hay and Eardisley — served as terminal stations for two of that Company's branch lines.

After considerable problems and struggles, the little Company was taken over by the Midland Railway on 1 October 1869 — even though that Company had no line of its own nearer than at Abbot's Wood just outside Worcester. However, as related in Chapter 1, the MR had subscribed towards the construction of the W&HR and had been allowed special facilities for its traffic (or conditional running powers) over that line. From 16 November 1868, MR goods trains ran between Worcester and Hereford, while from 1 July 1869, there were also four passenger trains in each direction. The latter service ceased on 1 November 1872, and it was not until 1 July 1896 that further MR passenger trains used the Worcester to Hereford line, and then only as far as Malvern, there being a daily through train in each direction between Birmingham (New Street) and Malvern which lasted until 1917.

The HH&BR had their own station at Hereford, making the third for that small city, this being at Moorfields, not far from the Barton premises of the NA&HR. From 1 April 1874, the MR's services to and from Brecon used Barton station, Moorfields being relegated to goods traffic. When in turn, from 2 January 1893, Barton ceased to be used for passenger trains (the last GWR trains having deserted it some 20 years previously) and became a goods station, the Brecon service was transferred to Barr's Court. By that time, however, it had been extended into a Hereford and Swansea through service, the MR having taken over the working of much of the Neth & Brecon's lines and absorbed the Swansea Vale Railway in 1874. Through carriages between Birmingham (New Street) and Swansea were run on two trains each day, being worked between Worcester and Hereford as part of a GWR train.

## The London & North Western Railway

Rather surprisingly, the LNWR which was usually the 'fly in the ointment' as far as the GWR was concerned, provided a most useful and necessary section of line at Hereford. This was from Rothewas Junction, on the GWR's Gloucester line, to Red Hill Junction on the line from Barton to Newport. This allowed through running between Shrewsbury and Newport through Barr's Court station. However, this line was not provided by the LNWR with altruistic motives, but to make it easier for the exercise of its running powers. Using the GWR's line to Gloucester, which was doubled as far as Rotherwas Junction, it had only two miles of track to construct — and allowing the GWR to use those two miles ensured that there would be no objection to its use of the GWR's line! The full benefits of this line became apparent some years later, when Barton station was closed to passengers and when the through services between the North and West of England were introduced, using Barr's Court station.

# 3 The West Midland Railway and The West Midland Section

**The West Midland Railway**

On 1 July 1860, the 'Old Worse and Worse', together with the Newport, Abergavenny & Hereford and the Worcester & Hereford Railways, ceased to exist. In their place was the West Midland Railway — promptly nicknamed the 'Werry Middling' — with a total mileage of just over 173 miles. 111 miles of this were contributed by the OW&WR, 52 miles by the NA&HR and just under 10 miles by the far from completed W&HR. All this was on the standard gauge, though two miles between Priestfield Junction and Cannock Road, Wolverhampton were mixed for the benefit of the GWR. Although the new Company was only to have a life of three years and one month, an additional 109 miles of line had been opened when, on 1 August 1863, it became part of the GWR.

At its birth it consisted of two as yet unconnected systems, the line from Worcester to Hereford being open only as far as Malvern Wells. The main work on the remaining section to Shelwick Junction was well under way — including the two tunnels at Malvern and Ledbury — while the Aberdare extension of the NA&HR was also in the course of construction. In addition to these lines, the Company was interested, under agreements either to work or to lease, in a number of other railways which were either authorised or already being constructed.

The Chairman of the WMR was William Fenton, late Chairman of the OW&WR with W. P. Price (former Chairman of the NA&HR) as Deputy Chairman. At first, relations with the GWR remained much as they had been since the Agreement of 1858, with practically all the London traffic passing over the LNWR by way of Yarnton and Bletchley. But events were to happen which changed all this.

In the autumn of 1860 the old proposal for a 'Mid Western' direct line from Yarnton to London was again revived, being brought before the public by unknown promoters who were backed by Lord Carrington and some other local people who had previously been active in support of the defeated projects of 1852 and 1853. As soon as the proposal was made known, Fenton wrote to the Chairman of the GWR and the LNWR assuring them that his Company had nothing to do with the proposal. The 1858 Agreement

**18**
'Sir Daniel' class 2-2-2 No 471 *Sir Watkin*, as rebuilt at Swindon in 1889. The class worked over the West Midland Section for much of their lives, and No 471 was one of seven engines whose final years were spent working from Oxford shed. *Real Photos*

provided that neither Company should in any way assist any new line competing with the other, so that the WMR was — so far — acting in accordance with the Agreement.

However, two months later Fenton complained that the GWR was assisting the Wycombe Railway in the promotion of a Bill for the extension of their line from Thames to Oxford — and that his Board considered this to be hostile to their 'well recognised position and prospects' as it would occupy 'the ground known to Railwaymen as the Mid Western District' (this being

on the strength of Parson's defeated projects of 1852 and 1853).

In reply the GWR stated that as the line was only a local branch, and could not possibly compete in any way with the WMR's main line, that Company's contention was invalid. He also pointed out that the only line with which it *could* possibly compete was the GWRs own line to Oxford! The response was to suggest that the Thame to Oxford proposal be withdrawn in return for the withdrawal of the Yarnton to London proposal. The GWR Chairman, Lord

**19**

2-4-0 No 376 of the Wolverhampton-built '111' class,
as rebuilt in 1894. This engine was shedded at
Hereford for many years until withdrawn in 1904.
*W. H. Whitworth/Real Photos*

**20**

'Dean Goods' No 2350 in original condition, one of
the many engines of the class which went as new to the
West Midland section. To the rear is one of the special
Droitwich salt vans in a train headed by Midland
Railway No 281, a Kirtley 0-6-0. By a strange
coincidence, the GWR's No 281 was also a Kirtley
0-6-0 and was used on the Droitwich salt trains.
*Real Photos*

Shelburne, declined to consider this as the Company
had agreements with the Wycombe Railway which it
was obliged to honour: he also expressed surprise that
the WMR were in any position to be able to offer to
withdraw a scheme with which they claimed to have
no interest!

It was then revealed that on the very day that
Fenton had written inviting the GWR to withdraw the
Thame to Oxford line, the WMR Board 'yielding to
great pressure on the part of the public' (!) had
adopted the line and made 'such arrangements with
the promoters as practically gave us a control over the
Bill'. This was treachery indeed, and on a scale worthy
of the 'Old Worse and Worse'; it seemed to indicate
that a change of name had not been accompanied by a
change of character!

The London, Buckinghamshire & West Midland
Junction Railway Bill was accordingly proceeded with.
Both sides drew up their forces for yet another battle.
On the one side was the WMR and the promoters of
the new line, while on the other was the unusual
alliance of the GWR and the LNWR: the latter was
never averse at aiding the discomforture of Paddington, but in this case it feared the infiltration of the
LSWR over the proposed new line. Then came the
astounding news that there would be no battle after all;
the 'impossible' had happened, for not only had the
GWR and the WMR settled their differences, but they
were to be amalgamated! The Bill was withdrawn and
by 4 May 1861, the Heads of Agreement between the
Boards of the two Companies were concluded. How
the LNWR viewed all this has not been recorded!

Under the Agreement, the original OW&WR line
was to be leased to the GWR (this still being legally
possible under the power of the Act of 1845) and that
company was to have running powers over and use of
the remainder of the WMR system. The two systems
were to be worked as far as possible as one unified
whole, the net receipts being divided into the pro-
portion of $82\frac{1}{2}$ to the GWR and $17\frac{1}{2}$ to the WMR. A
Joint Committee of 18 GWR Directors and six from
the WMR were to manage the whole undertaking.

The narrow gauge was to be completed from
Reading to Paddington and Brentford (A Bill for the
necessary powers to do this was already in Parliament), so as to be ready for traffic, if possible, on the
opening of the W&HR and Severn Valley lines. After
this, express trains were to be worked over the two
systems as if they were one. Within five years application was to be made to Parliament for a amalgamation of the two Companies. The Lease and Agreement were
to begin from 1 July 1861.

The alliance between the GWR and the LNWR was
soon dissolved as one of the casualties of the new
Agreement was Parson's Agreement with Captain
Huish in 1853, which had tied the OW&WR to the
LNWR for 21 years. It was not enforcable by law, and
as early as 1856 some of the OW&WR's Directors
had been complaining that Euston had been neglecting
the terms. One of the clauses had been that the LNWR
would help the smaller Company to obtain a direct
route to London, so that the LNWR's opposition to
the Buckinghamshire project was a definite breach of
Agreement — and provided a ready-made reason for
abandoning it!

However, the London service to and from Euston
continued until the end of September, as there was no
means of running through trains to and from Paddington. In October, Paddington finally became the
London station for the Worcester services and for
those to and from the WMR in general. The Yarnton
loop remained in situ and was used for the transfer of
goods traffic, not least during the war years when it
assumed an unexpected importance.

There were six lines in which the WMR had been
interested at the time of its formation. The Severn
Valley Railway extended from Hartlebury to
Shrewsbury (a distance of almost 40 miles) and connected with this line were two smaller lines; the Much
Wenlock & Severn Junction Railway, from Buildwas
to the town of Much Wenlock, three and a half miles
away, and the Tenbury & Bewdley Railway, from
Bewdley to the existing terminus of the Tenbury
Railway, a distance of 15 miles. Much further to the
south, the Witney Railway was to run from Yarnton to
Witney, a distance of eight miles; while the Bourton-
on-the-Water Railway was to connect that small town
to the main line at Chipping Norton Junction, six and
a half miles away. Finally, to the north, there was the
Stourbridge Railway, from Stourbridge Junction to
Old Hill, a distance of three and a half miles.

For the next two years the WMR, though working
in the closest co-operation with the GWR, retained its

21

own individuality (not least in the matter of loco-motives) and was managed by its own officers — though under the Joint Committee. This was largely due to the uncertainty over sanction being given by Parliament to the proposed amalgamation, which it was thought would be strongly opposed by the LNWR and by the MR.

Within months of its formation, the WMR had shown that it had not lost some of the 'Old Worse and Worse' dreams of expansion, and in 1861 had nearly gained control of the Monmouthshire Railway. Although the attempt was not renewed, the WMR succeeded, in spite of strong opposition from the Monmouthshire in getting statutory running powers between Coedygric Junction and Newport — a line over which the NA&HR's trains had alway worked, though only by agreement with the owning Company. An unexpected — and far from welcome — con-sequence of this apparent triumph on the part of the WMR was the arrival in Newport of LNWR trains! That Company had for long set its sights on the prize of better access to the black gold of Monmouthshire's collieries, and made an agreement with the Monmouthshire Railway in August 1863 — when the latter Company was obviously feeling threatened and seeking a strong ally. By this Agreement, the LNWR were given running powers for all kinds of traffic to Newport (having already got running powers between Hereford and Pontypool Road). As well as goods trains, there was one passenger train each way until the end of 1865. When the Monmouthshire was absor-bed by the GWR in 1876, the latter Company inherited the LNWR presence in Newport as a 'cuckoo in the nest'.

**21**
No 2326 was another engine which went as new to the West Midlands and spent its entire life there. It is seen here at Worcester shed, fitted with a Belpaire boiler.
*W. H. Whitworth/Real Photos*

**22**
0-6-0ST No 1532 as built at Wolverhampton in 1879. This was one of a number of such engines which was shedded at Stourbridge for many years. Rebuilt as a pannier tank in 1921, it was withdrawn in 1948.
*Real Photos*

**23**
'517' class 0-4-2T No 834 at Worcester c1882. The ex-OW&WR Kirtley 0-6-0 No 281 is in the rear.
*Real Photos*

The first new line was that of the final section of the W&HR, providing at long last direct communication between the two cities, this taking place on 17 Septem-ber 1861. The main engineering works were the Malvern and Ledbury Tunnels, 1,567yd and 1,323yds respectively, and the Ledbury Viaduct. This was followed on 18 November by the opening of the Witney Railway. Prior to these events, the $16\frac{1}{4}$ miles of the Colefore, Monmouth, Usk & Pontypool Railway had been added to the WMRs total on 1 July when that line was absorbed. The following year saw the opening of several new lines, of which the most important was the Severn Valley Railway to Shrewsbury, opened on 1 February; the Much

30

Wenlock Railway was opened at the same time. A month later, on 1 March, the Bourton-on-the-Water branch was opened for traffic.

On 1 July 1862, the S&HR became the joint property of the LNWR, GWR and WMR Companies, and on the same day the Leominster & Kington Railway became part of the WMR. It had been opened in August 1857 and worked by the contractor, Brassey, until taken over jointly by the WMR and GWR. (For some reason the LNWR either 'missed out' on this occasion or were not interested in getting a share.) Finally, two miles of the Stourbridge Railway to Cradley were opened in April 1863.

The only other line opened during the WMR's short existence was a short extension of the Stratford-on-Avon branch to join the GWR's branch from Hatton, which took place in August 1861. Although a short length of line, it was of considerable importance; it made possible a through service between Leamington and Worcester, which at first was extended to Malvern, and nearly half a century later it became part of the new route from Birmingham to South Wales and the West of England via Cheltenham.

The Bill for amalgamation of the WMR and the GWR met strenuous opposition, though it was eventually passed. The Act came into force on 1 August 1863, the WMR being dissolved on that date.

22

23

At the time of dissolution, the WMR owned about 180 miles of line, as well as the more-or-less defunct Stratford & Moreton Tramway, and leased or worked another 77 miles. The whole of the West Midland Section as it became, apart from the Chipping Norton and Stratford branches, was laid with bridge rail on longitudinal timbers, while most of the former NA&HR consisted of Barlow rails. On the former OW&WR line there were no less than 76 timber viaducts and bridges, all north of Evesham, most of which had to be renewed during the next 20 years. The Chairman of the WMR, W. Fenton became the Deputy Chairman of the GWR, while six WMR Directors were elected to join the GWR Board.

**The West Midland Section**
Hardly had the WMR been safely gathered into the GWR fold when trouble arose at the southern extremity of its former territory. Some influential residents of Cheltenham, feeling that their town was badly treated by the GWR, joined with certain Gloucestershire landowners to promote the East Gloucestershire Railway. As well as a line from Cheltenham to Faringdon, there was to be a branch

24

25

26

**24**

Half a century later, No 834 was still at Worcester in 1932 — though considerably altered by rebuilding. A 'Dean Goods' is to the rear. *J. A. H. G. Coltas*

**25**

No 6388 on an engineering train entering Evesham in 1956. The engine shed is above the train, between the main line and the LMS line to Ashchurch. *R. C. Riley*

**26**

No 3821 on a freight train from Hereford uses the Worcester avoiding line, while a laden coal train from South Wales to the Midlands passes on the other line. 1956. *R. C. Riley*

from Fairford to the existing terminus of the Witney Railway. Agreement having been reached with the GWR and the WMR, who undertook to subscribe a large portion of the capital, to substitute a branch from Andoversford to Bourton-on-the-Water for that to Witney. Although sanctioned by Parliament, the GWR shareholders disregarded their Directors' advice and resolved 'that the East Gloucestershire Railway be abandoned'.

The EGR then made a new application, for its original lines, with connections at Cheltenham to both the GWR and the MR. When the EGR not only reduced the provision for broad gauge track in their proposal, but accepted an offer from the MR to subscribe £10,000 and work the line on easy terms, the GWR was 'not amused'. This was real aggression, which would have brought the MR almost to Swindon! It was considered to be a breach of an Agreement between the two Companies in respect of the 1863 Act for the WMR and GWR amalgamation. When both the right of the MR to subscribe to the EGR and to work it were rejected by the Board of Trade, the EGR was forced to come to terms with the GWR. Their line as constructed was nothing more than an extension of the Witney Railway to Fairford.

Further north, an event of considerable consequence — as well as being of not a little local excitement — was the complete destruction by fire of the carriage shops at Worcester. These were burnt to the ground, and 18 new carriages in them destroyed, on the night of 12 November 1864. This helped to speed the decision to establish a central carriage works at Swindon in place of the three existing works at Paddington (for broad gauge stock), at Saltney (the former S&CR works) and at Worcester.

New lines opened during the first few years after the amalgamation included a connection between the former NA&HR's line at Quaker's Yard and that of the Vale of Neath at Middle Duffryn Junction in 1864. The opening of the Tenbury & Bewdley Railway following in August; while further north on the Severn Valley line, a short extension of the Much Wenlock

**27**
An ex-West Midland 2-4-0 and train near Bransford Road, c1890. *Bucknall Collection/IAL*

**28**
The north end of Shrub Hill station, with No 5816 entering on a train from Leominster. No 1418 stands on the centre line, while a third 0-4-2T stands in the bay on a train to Leominster. 26 June 1950. *Author*

Railway from Buildwas Junction to Coalbrookdale was opened on 1 November — thus making possible a through service between Wellington and Much Wenlock. A few weeks later a further extension of the Wenlock Railway, this time from Much Wenlock westwards to Presthope, was opened during the following month; and a final section of 11 miles from Presthope to Marsh Farm Junction on the S&HR line was to be opened three years later in December 1867, making a complete branch of nearly 30 miles from Wellington to Craven Arms.

The Stourbridge Railway opened further short sections of line in 1866 and 1867; on the same day as the second of these was opened (1 April 1867) to join the LNWR at Galton Junction, a vital line — though only three quarters of a mile long — came into use from Smethwick Junction (near Galton Junction) to Handsworth Junction on the main line between Birmingham and Wolverhampton. This made it possible to run through services between Birmingham, Worcester and Hereford — and eventually South Wales. An even shorter, but well-known, branch was opened at Worcester in 1872, this being the famous 'Vinegar Branch' to the premises of Hill, Evans & Co.

1874 saw the beginnings of a branch which was to take over 20 years to complete, which must have been a record for a line only 24 miles long! The first section of the Worcester, Bromyard & Leominster Railway, whose purpose was as indicated by its title, was the seven miles from Bromyard Junction, on the Worcester to Hereford line, to Yearsett on 2 May. A further three years passed before any further progress was made, the four miles to Bromyard being opened on 22 May 1877.

Although not part of the West Midland Section, the opening of the Pontypool, Caerleon & Newport Railway, on 17 September 1874, must be mentioned. This provided direct access to Newport and the South Wales main line (which had been converted to standard gauge in 1872) from the former NA&HR line at Pontypool, thus making possible the introduction of a through service between Birmingham and Cardiff. The following year saw the opening of two rural lines in Herefordshire and Radnor; the first of these, from Titley to Presteign, was a branch of the existing Leominster & Kington Railway; the other, although an extension of the latter's line to the small village of New Radnor, was actually a detached section of another railway, the Kington & Eardisley, whose 'main' line from Titley to Eardisley had opened on 3 August 1874.

An important, though short, line was opened on 1 June 1878, this being from Kidderminster Junction to Bewdley, thus providing direct access from Kidderminster to both the Severn Valley line and that from Bewdley to Tenbury and Woofferton. In later years both lines tended to have their services based on Kidderminster rather than on Hartlebury or Worcester. The triangle of lines thus created also enabled the GWR to dispense with the turntable at Kidderminster shed in 1899 — though the eight and a half miles of 'light engine' running involved must have been both time-consuming and expensive. The even shorter branch from Stourbridge Junction to Stourbridge Town, with a length of only 73 chains, was opened for traffic on 1 October 1879.

Three years later, on 1 June 1881, the first section of the Banbury & Cheltenham Direct Railway was opened, this being an extension of the existing Bourton-on-the-Water branch to Lansdown Junction, Cheltenham (fulfilling the abortive proposal made in connection with the EGR in 1863). The northern section also consisted of an extension of an existing branch line, this being the Chipping Norton branch which was extended to King's Sutton on the Oxford to Banbury main line, though this was not opened until 6 April 1887. Even then, through running was not possible without reversal at Chipping Norton Junction; the direct loop line avoiding the station did not come into use until 1906, shortly after which event Chipping Norton Junction was renamed Kingham.

1884 saw another chapter in the history — or saga — of the Worcester, Bromyard & Leominster Railway, this time the new section was opened from the Leominster end where just under four miles of line were opened as far as Steens Bridge on 1 March. However, it was not until 1 September 1897, that the intervening nine miles between Steens Bridge and Bromyard were opened. 27 July 1885, brought the opening of another cross-country branch between Gloucester and Ledbury; for many years through trains were run over this line between Gloucester and Worcester.

The almost derelict Stratford & Moreton Tramway was reconstructed as a branch line in 1889, when the Shipston-on-Stour branch was opened. Apart from the final section of the Worcester, Bromyard & Leominster, already mentioned, there were no more additions until 1901. In that year the Stourbridge Town branch was altered and extended when a new station was opened at Stourbridge Junction to the south of the old station.

Also in 1901, the GWR re-opened the Golden Valley Railway, from Pontrilas to Hay (on the MR's line from Hereford to Brecon). This was an impecunious and rather ramshackle line which had been opened in 1881 from Pontrilas to Dorstone and extended to Hay in 1889. Owing to great financial problems, it was closed in sections (in reverse order to these being opened) in 1897 and 1898. Although the GWR acquired the line on 1 July 1899, services did not recommence until 1 May 1901, this being due in part to the generally run-down condition of the line.

The first few years of this century saw a great period of GWR 'short cuts' and new lines, among these being the opening of a new line from Honeybourne to Cheltenham which made possible the introduction of new through services between Birmingham and South Wales and the West of England. The first section from Honeybourne to Broadway was opened in 1904, when the East and North Junctions at Honeybourne were also opened: this involved considerable reconstruction at Honeybourne station and the demolition of the engine shed. Although it was resited, it was burnt down a short time afterwards: as the GWR decided not to risk a repeat performance, engines were stabled in the open for the next 40 years. The line was opened throughout to Cheltenham (Malvern Road) in 1906. In the same year, the new direct loop at Chipping Norton Junction was opened on 8 January and a few years later a through service between the north-east of England and South Wales began running over what was now correctly named — the Banbury & Cheltenham Direct Line.

Considerable alterations and extensions were made at many stations over the years. Chipping Norton Junction was extensively altered and enlarged when the Banbury and Cheltenham lines were opened; new junctions being provided for both the Chipping Norton and Bourton lines, as well as extra platforms, while the main line platforms were lengthened. An engine shed was provided near the junction in 1881, this being replaced by another building in 1913. At Evesham the alterations involved the removal of the original OW&WR engine shed — this being an unusual building as part of its roof and walls were formed by an overhead bridge! A new engine shed was provided to the north of the station in 1901.

As might be expected, some of the greatest changes took place at Worcester itself, though Shrub Hill joint station (the MR had their own booking office and staff) saw little change between 1882 and 1925, apart from the loss of its original overall roof. The Locomotive Works were greatly improved and enlarged, and new carriage shops replaced those which had been burnt down — these resembled a row of large north-light greenhouses! There were great changes at Kidderminster over the years, both platforms being lengthened, the goods station greatly enlarged, and in 1932 a new engine shed provided to take the place of the ancient wooden structure dating back to the early days of the 'Old Worse and Worse'. Fortunately, the splendid timbered facade of the main station building remained unchanged.

Having had a new station in 1901, Stourbridge Junction was provided with a new engine shed in 1926 — the original having been built in 1870, when it replaced the old OW&WR shed at Dudley. However, the old shed found a new use as a shed for rail motors and later for diesel railcars, and in 1944 was re-opened as an engine shed to deal with the greatly increased wartime freight traffic. The old shed at Dudley was taken down and thriftilly re-erected elsewhere in the neighbourhood as a grain shed. Perhaps the greatest changes took place at Wolverhampton, where the original overall roof was replaced by platform canopies, the layout considerably altered and improved, and the former OW&WR engine shed demolished — the latter taking place as early as 1864,

when the engines were transferred to the Stafford Road sheds.

There was also the replacement of the numerous wooden viaducts and bridges on the main line, the best-known of these being Churchill — which was 173yd long. The lofty structure of wood, carried on stone pillars, at Stourbridge, was also replaced by a stone one. The greatest example of bridge replacement was at Worcester, where the iron bridge across the Severn was renewed in 1905.

Between Worcester and Hereford, improvements to the line included the doubling of the former single line sections, that between Malvern and Shelwick Junction being finished in July 1860, with the exception of the Malvern and Ledbury Tunnels. Although some alterations were made in the layout at Malvern (Great) — for thus the GWR insisted in was — the station buildings remained virtually unaltered as a superb example of Victorian semi-ecclesiastical architecture (usually associated with cemetery chapels rather than with railway stations!). All that was lacking was a tower or spire, though the roof was crowned with an amazing erection having eight pinnacles in addition to a central fleche surmounted by a weather vane: this was a clock tower, having four clock faces. There were cast-iron embellishments on all the roof ridges, including several gables, while the lamp standards in the forecourt were ornamented with cast-iron scroll work. The glazed awning under which cabs — and later taxis — embarked or discharged passengers was a disappointing exception to this splendid ensemble.

One of the earlier improvement schemes was undertaken at Barr's Court, Hereford, where the original mixed gauge station with its overall roof was swept away and replaced by a much larger set of premises. A few miles to the north, a major improvement scheme was carried out at the beginning of this century at Leominster. Not only were the main platforms almost doubled in length, but what amounted to a new goods yard was constructed at the south end of the station; this brought about the demolition of the old engine shed, which was replaced by a similar building at the north end of the station. The most striking feature of Leominster station was without doubt the signalbox which was situated on the island platform, standing high on a single line of supports and firmly anchored in place by horizontal girders which stretched across the lines and were firmly anchored to another set of uprights on the branch platform. The whole creation was undoubtedly of LNWR design, and was a reminder that this was a Joint Line!

On 1 January 1922, the GWR took over the little Cleobury Mortimer & Ditton Priors Light Railway, which was but 12 miles long and had been opened for only 14 years. Running from Cleobury Junction, on the Tenbury & Bewdley Railway, up the course of the

**29**

Enginemen going on duty pause for a brief chat at the end of the up platform at Worcester, Shrub Hill, while 0-6-0PT No 2094 emerges from shunting the 'Hereford Sidings'. In the distance, an 0-4-2T with auto-trailer stands in front of the through shed. 26 June 1950. *Author*

**30**

2-6-2T No 4153 on a Worcester to Ledbury train crosses the canal bridge between Shrub Hill and Foregate Street stations at Worcester. *R. J. Doran*

River Rea to Ditton Priors, its primary purpose was to provide rail access for the granite quarries at Abdon Clee — though it did also convey passengers and goods traffic. The passenger service was withdrawn in 1938, but freight traffic continued — largely due to the building of a large Admiralty depot near the terminus. Its two Manning Wardle 0-6-0STs, *Burwarton* and *Cleobury*, rebuilt with pannier tanks as GWR Nos 28 and 29, were for many years familiar engines in the Kidderminster area.

The Kingswinsford goods branch which had been opened from Brettell Lane (then known as Kingswins-ford Junction) in 1858, was extended to Dunstall Park, just north of Wolverhampton in the early 1920s — a triangular junction being made with the northern main line. This not only provided a route for through freight traffic in connection with the Oxley yard, but was also used for a new Wolverhampton 'suburban' service to and from Stourbridge Junction, this being worked by rail motors. However, the latter did not last very long. Also withdrawn in the 1920s was the passenger service on the Shipston-on-Stour branch, which was with-drawn as from 8 July 1929, though a goods service of a limited kind was to outlast the GWR itself.

# 4    West Midland Locomotives

**Oxford, Worcester & Wolverhampton Railway**
The first sections of the OW&WR being worked by the MR, it was not until May 1852, when there was a continuous line from Evesham to Stourbridge, that the Company required locomotives of its own. Even then, the line was worked by contract by C. C. Williams, with David Joy (of Joy's valve gear fame) as his Superintendent. By October 1854 the whole of the main line from Wolvercot Junction to Bushbury Junction was ready for use, and the locomotive stock provided by Williams was already proving quite inadequate. The Company was forced into buying engines of their own and hiring others from the LNWR, while much of the traffic between Handborough and Worcester was being worked by the latter Company.

William's contract was terminated on 1 February 1856, and his stock of 27 engines was taken over at valuation. David Joy was replaced by Frederic Haward, who had already been acting for the Company, whilst from 1857 Edward Wilson was in charge. Prior to this, the workshops at Worcester had been opened early in 1854, though it was some time before they were properly equipped.

When the WMR was formed in 1860, the OW&WR engines retained their numbers 1-59. Edward Wilson became the Locomotive Superintendent of the new Company, remaining in charge of the West Midland Section after the 1863 amalgamation. However, all major repairs were carried out at Wolverhampton, and for the next 30 years Worcester played a very minor role. With Hereford and Kidderminster, Worcester formed a District within the Northern Division — completely dominated by Wolverhampton.

David Joy's appointment had been made only a fortnight before the opening from Evesham to Stourbridge, and he was only able to obtain six locomotives prior to the line being opened. These, which he designated A to F instead of the more usual practice of numbering, had to suffice until engines on order from

R. & W. Hawthorn began to be delivered later in the year.

'A' was a 2-4-0 tender engine built by E. B. Wilson & Co in 1849, and was purchased from a firm of contractors at Pontefract. Joy converted it to a 2-2-2 at Worcester in October 1853. It later became OW&WR No 31. 'B' was a long-boiler 0-6-0 built by R. Stephenson & Co, obtained from contractors to the Great Northern Railway at Offord: it had a limited life, disappearing by 1854. 'C' was an 0-4-2, also by Wilson's, with outside frames, and bore the name *Canary*; consideration was given to this engine being taken into stock in 1854, but it was finally rejected.

'D' and 'E' were also long-boiler tender engines, of the 2-4-0 type, built by Kitson, Thompson & Hewitson in 1849, which were borrowed from the North Staffordshire Railway and returned in 1852. 'F' — which was also known as *Mudlark* — was also purchased from contractors to the GNR, this time at Welwyn, and had disappeared by 1854. Several other engines were reported to have worked on the line for short periods, but few details are known.

Hawthorn's delivered the first locomotives to be built for the OW&WR — 12 passenger and eight goods — in 1852; the passenger engines carrying the numbers 1-5 and 11-17, while the goods engines were Nos 6-10 and 18-20. The former were 2-4-0s, with double frames (the outside being of sandwich pattern), 5ft 9in wheels and 16in + 20in cylinders. Joy mentions that No 1 was the first engine he remembered with a weatherboard in place of a completely open footplate, so the Company deserves a little credit for its contribution to the comfort of enginemen! These engines later became GWR Nos 171-81 (No 13 having been withdrawn in 1860).

Nos 171-5 were never rebuilt and all were withdrawn by 1885. Nos 176 and 179 were rebuilt at Worcester in 1864, receiving new boilers, and lasted until 1886 and 1881 respectively. No 177 was put

**31**
The first engine owned by the OW&WR, 2-4-0 No 1, built by Hawthorns in 1852; in original condition as GWR No 171. Withdrawn in 1885. *Real Photos*

**32**
A WMR (ex-OW&WR) 2-4-0 built by Wilson's, at Evesham in 1863. *Real Photos*

down to work the Worcester sawmill (for the Carriage Works) in January 1857, but by 1864 its tube plate was in such a bad condition that another engine was also put down to the same work. No 177 was withdrawn in 1865, but later re-instated, overhauled and returned to traffic: it lasted until October 1880. Nos 178, 180 and 181 were all rebuilt at Wolverhampton between 1871 and 1875, when they received new inside frames and 'Metro' class boilers; they were again rebuilt with similar boilers between 1889 and 1892, being withdrawn between 1899 and 1902. The class generally remained at Worcester and Hereford,

33

34

35

**33**

GWR No 184 began life as OW&WR No 23, being built by Wilson's in 1853. Seen here in early rebuilt condition. *Real Photos*

**34**

Rebuilt again, as seen here at Worcester, No 184 was withdrawn in 1899. *Real Photos*

**35**

One of the few OW&WR express passenger engines, No 41 was built by Wilson's in 1855. Seen here in original condition, as GWR No 189, it was withdrawn in 1886. *Bucknall Collection/IAL*


though some were reported from Shrewsbury and Pontypool Road.

The corresponding goods engines were of the same general design, with 5ft 0in wheels and 17in + 24in cylinders. Nos 7 and 19 were early withdrawals and were replaced by new engines in 1860-1. The remainder became GWR Nos 239, 241-3, 245 and 247, and were withdrawn between 1878 and 1885, with the exception of No 245 (old No 18). The latter engine was twice rebuilt; in December 1876, at Swindon, with a Wolverhampton 'Standard Goods' boiler; and in February 1893, at Wolverhampton, with a Swindon boiler of the same type. In the latter form it lasted until December 1902. The last days of No 243 were spent at Worcester, as pilot engine, where it was generally known to all and sundry as 'Mother Shuter'; it was withdrawn in October 1878.

The three withdrawn engines were replaced by new engines erected at Worcester, probably from parts obtained elsewhere, in 1860-1, and very similar in appearance to the MR double-framed goods engines of the period (of which the WMR had 12). Nos 240 and 246 (old Nos 7 and 8) were withdrawn in 1884-5, but No 244 was renewed with new frames and altered wheelbase in January 1877, lasting until May 1902.

Another lot of 2-4-0 engines, with a similar pattern of double frames, were delivered by E. B. Wilson & Co in 1853. Nos 21-6 (GWR Nos 182-7) had 5ft 8in wheels and 16in + 20in cylinders. No 187 was a fairly early withdrawal in 1886, but the others were twice rebuilt and lasted much longer. All had cabs added in the 1870s, and later closed splashers replaced the early slotted varieties. They were finally withdrawn between 1897 and 1904, No 186 (shedded at Worcester) having run a total of 1,075,744 miles in service.

No 31 was the former 'A', rebuilt as a 2-2-2 in 1855 and was withdrawn in 1876 as GWR No 206. Two additional 2-4-0s and two 0-6-0s delivered by Wilson's in 1853 became Nos 27-30; but these were sold in

March 1854 to the GNR, having been built to the design of their Superintendent, Sturrock.

The following year Wilson's delivered four double-framed 0-6-0s, a fifth engine of this class following in 1855. They received the Nos 27-30 and 34 (GWR Nos 248-52) and had 5ft 3in wheels — though No 28 had 5ft 0in wheels — and 16in + 24in cylinders. No 248 was rebuilt at Worcester in 1864 and withdrawn in 1886, while No 249 (with smaller wheels) was never rebuilt and lasted only until 1877. However, the others lasted much longer, all being rebuilt, having had different boilers on successive rebuilds. No 250 actually managed a third rebuild in 1902, but all were withdrawn between 1903 and 1907.

Nos 32 and 33 (GWR Nos 278 and 279) were inside-framed 0-6-0s built by Wilson's in 1854-5, being described as ballast engines. They had 4ft 6in wheels and 16in + 24in cylinders. Neither was rebuilt, No 278 being withdrawn in 1878; though No 279 survived a few years longer, and was withdrawn in 1885 after working for some years at Shrewsbury. Nos 35 and 36 (GWR Nos 221 and 222) were diminutive 0-4-2 saddle tanks delivered by Wilson's in November 1853 (despite the peculiar numbering sequence). They had 3ft 5in coupled wheels, with trailing wheels of 3ft 0in and cylinders $9\frac{1}{4}$in + 14in. The boilers were domeless, with a raised casing over the firebox, and the short tank covered the boiler barrel only. With a grate area of only 6.72sq ft their total heating surface was a mere 263sq ft. They were sold out of service in 1872-3.

The next three engines were acquired second-hand from the Manchester, Sheffield & Lincolnshire Railway in October 1854. Double-framed 0-6-0s, they were almost new engines — having been built in 1852-3, the first two by Stephenson's and the third by Sharp, Stewart & Co. They had been Nos 110 *Himalaya*, 112 *Visto* and 118 *Pollux* while on the MS&LR and retained these numbers and names for some times after their arrival at Worcester. All were repaired by Beyer, Peacock & Co, in 1855. With 5ft 0in wheels and 18in + 24in cylinders, they were very powerful engines, but suffered from a serious defect: the trailing axle passed through a bridge in the firebox, which divided the grate into separate halves and was, in Joy's words, 'awful trouble, always leaking'. This may explain their early sale by their original owners, but that Company appears to have been prone at this time to dispose of almost new engines to a variety of other railways!

No 38 was sold in 1861 to the Ebbw Vale Co for £1,500 — payment being made in rails! Nos 37 and 39 became GWR Nos 237 and 238, but the latter never worked as such, being put down to work the Worcester sawmill early in 1861 and continued to do this until 1867. No 237 was rebuilt at Worcester in October 1865 as a saddle tank, and received new 17in cylinders in 1878; still with the original troublesome boiler, it was withdrawn in August 1885.

From the end of 1854 the locomotive situation became increasingly alarming. A report by John Fowler, the Engineer, dated 2 December 1854, disclosed the parlous state of the stock: of the 31 engines reviewed, only 11 were in good condition; all the others being either under repair or in need of repairs. Not only were the LNWR working the passenger trains south of Worcester, they had also hired at least four goods engines to the Company. The condition of the overworked stock went on deteriorating and matters reached a climax in a series of mishaps near Hartlebury on the night of 18 October 1855.

From Worcester the 6.45pm train from Oxford to Wolverhampton should have had engine No 24 (a Wilson 2-4-0 of 1853), but the regulator had failed in bringing in the 6.00pm Wolverhampton to Worcester. The driver was obliged to carry on with No 14 (a Hawthorn 2-4-0) which had brought the train from Oxford. At Hartlebury the tyre of the near trailing wheel jammed against the firebox, whereupon the Stationmaster telegraphed to Kidderminster for another engine. No 25 (another Wilson 2-4-0) was sent to the rescue, but on nearing Hartlebury the driver saw warning lights, reversed — and *'lost his regulator'*. Having no means of shutting off steam, he proceeded to Worcester and reported the situation!

Joy himself then started off as soon as possible on No 10 (a Hawthorn 2-4-0) and managed to get to Hartlebury without mishap; however, just as he was ready to start off with the train the gauge glass broke and, when he attempted to shut off steam from the gauge, one of the studs blew out! Another engine from Worcester (number not recorded) took the train on at 3.00am, 6hr 8min late, after a delay of about five and a half hours!

There can have been little regret for either the Company or the Contractor when the contract was terminated on 1 February 1856. However, David Joy was out of employment — and Haward was left with a load of trouble on his hands.

In the summer of 1855, Wilson's had supplied two 2-4-0 *express* engines, Nos 40 and 41 (GWR Nos 188 and 189), with 6ft 6in wheels and 15½in + 22in cylinders. Despite their larger wheels, they were not so free-running as the 5ft 8in engines. No 188 was withdrawn, unaltered, in 1878; but No 189 was rebuilt at Hereford in July 1864, when it received new 15in + 22in cylinders — this being one of the very few records of any such work being undertaken at Hereford. It was again rebuilt, with 5ft 9in wheels, a cab, brass dome cover and other Wolverhampton details being fitted — in July 1882, though this was carried out at Worcester (despite that Works not being allowed to reboiler engines). No 41 appears to have

been 'the exception that proves the rule'. It was withdrawn in March 1886.

In 1856, a further 10 engines, of three types, were added to stock, all being built by Wilson's. Nos 42 and 51 (GWR Nos 207 and 208) were large 'Jenny Linds', No 51 being distinguished by carrying the name *Will Shakspere* (evidently a local spelling). The driving wheels were 6ft 3in and they had 15in + 22in cylinders. They worked mainly between Oxford and Worcester — initially on the Euston trains — and were withdrawn in March 1876 and December 1878 respectively, without being rebuilt.

Nos 43-6 were more double-framed 0-6-0s, with 5ft 0in wheels and 16in + 24in cylinders (GWR Nos 264-7), the last three being broken up, without any attempt being made at rebuilding, in 1878-9. However, No 264 was a very different case, as it was rebuilt or reboilered five times — in 1875, 1889, 1909, 1912 and 1914 — and was not withdrawn until June 1921, by which time it had achieved a mileage of 1,053,658. The first rebuild, in September 1875, was really a 'renewal' as it had new 17in + 24in cylinders as well as a new standard Wolverhampton boiler — not to mention the wheelbase being altered and increased by five inches! It also received a new number, being henceforth No 49. The other rebuildings were confined to fitting new boilers, the last of which was a Belpaire boiler.

Nos 47-50 were 0-6-0 back tanks, with inside frames, of a standard design — many of which were built for collieres in the North of England. They had 4ft 8in wheels and 15in + 20in cylinders, becoming GWR Nos 231-4. They worked around Worcester for the whole of their lives, being withdrawn between 1877 and 1880.

By 1859, when further engines were added to stock, the firm of E. B. Wilson & Co had ceased to exist, so that the Company had to turn elsewhere for additional engines. The first two of these, Nos 52 and 53, were small 2-2-2 well tanks of a somewhat exotic appearance which were built by Stephenson's. They had inside frames, outside cylinders, ornamental dome covers, and large cabs with side windows; the whole effect was to suggest that they had strayed across the Atlantic! The driving wheels were 5ft 6in and the carrying wheels 3ft 6in, with 12in + 18in cylinders. No 52 was named *Ben Johnson* (presumably to complement *Will Shakspere*') while No 53, although not named, was known as 'Mrs Johnson'! One of them was employed on working the first trains between Henwick and Malvern Link. They became GWR Nos 223 and 224, and worked on the branches from Chipping Norton Junction, being withdrawn in 1877-8.

In 1860 the Company took delivery of two Kirtley 0-6-0s from the MR which had been built a few

**36**

GWR No 192 was originally NA&HR No 29 *Elk* and for a brief period WMR No 95. Built in 1855, it was rebuilt at Wolverhampton in 1874 and 1890 — as seen here — and withdrawn in 1903.  *Real Photos*

**37**

An ex-S&HR 2-4-0 built by Vulcan Foundry in 1854, GWR No 219 lasted until 1876. Wolverhampton-built 2-4-0 of the '111' class, in original condition, is in the rear. 1863.  *Real Photos*

**38**

WMR 0-6-0 of the '27' class (ex-OW&WR), in original condition as built by Wilson's in 1854. *Real Photos*

37

38

months earlier at Derby. Nos 54 and 55 (GWR Nos 280 and 281) had the usual double frames, though the inside frames extended to the firebox only, 5ft 2in wheels — later reduced to 5ft 0in — and 16in + 24in cylinders. Apart from both engines receiving 17in cylinders, little alteration took place and they continued to work from Worcester on the Droitwich to London salt trains until withdrawn in 1884. Four other goods engines, all 0-6-0s, were also delivered in 1860, though they were of two distinct classes and built by different firms. Nos 56 and 57 (GWR Nos 296 and 297) were by Kitson's, having outside sandwich frames and inside plate frames which had bearings for the driving axle only, the wheels were 5ft 3in and cylinders 16$\frac{1}{2}$in + 24in. Both received 17in cylinders in 1877, but were not otherwise altered and they continued to work from Worcester until withdrawn in 1885-6.

Nos 58 and 59, the last engines delivered to the OW&WR, were by Stephenson's, being of that firm's standard pattern, with double frames, 5ft 3in wheels and 16in + 24in cylinders. They became GWR Nos 294 and 295, the latter engine being withdrawn from Worcester in 1882. No 294 received new 17in cylinders in December 1875, after which it worked mainly between Wolverhampton and Chester. In December 1889 it was rebuilt — though really this was a 'renewal' — with new frames, altered wheelbase, new boiler and 17$\frac{1}{2}$in cylinders, at the same time being renumbered 47. Although it now had the same type of boiler as No 49, renewed the previous month, the wheelbase was different. Like No 49, No 47 was

reboilered another four times — in 1902, 1908, 1911 and 1914 — though none of the boilers was identical with those fitted to the other engine, nor did No 47 every carry a Belpaire boiler. From 1890 it was shedded mainly at Wolverhampton or Shrewsbury, being withdrawn in April 1921 — two months before No 49. Like the latter engine, its total mileage was over a million miles.

**Newport, Abergavenny & Hereford Railway**
As in the case of the OW&WR, the Company at first owned no locomotives. For the first nine months it was worked by the LNWR, with Thomas Brassey apparently supplying the locomotives — and he continued to do so until the Company itself took over the working on 1 January 1855.

When the WMR was formed in 1860, the company possessed 26 engines, numbered (as far as is known) 1-22, 27-30: these were allotted WMR numbers 71-96 in progressive order, and all later became GWR property. The workshops were at Barton, Hereford, the Resident Engineer and Locomotive Superintendent being Mark Carr until October 1858, when Alexander McDonnell was appointed. Archibald Sturrock, of the GNR, appears to have been chief advisor on locomotive matters. Apart from three built by Dodds & Co, all the engines were built by Wilson's, who had quite a 'Corner' in the engine market for the West Midland lines.

Two classes of 0-6-0 tender engines were delivered between 1854 and 1858, the first consisting of Nos 1-6 and 10 (GWR Nos 253-6, 268) which had the usual

**39**

GWR No 252 was another 0-6-0 built by Wilson's for the OW&WR in 1855. Rebuilt, as seen here, with 'Sir Daniel' class boiler in 1891, it was withdrawn in 1904. *Real Photos*

**40**

Stephenson's built GWR No 295 in 1860, as OW&WR No 59. It was withdrawn in 1882, without rebuilding; however, its 'twin' No 58 (GWR No 294) was rebuilt four times and lasted until 1921! *Real Photos*

**41**

GWR No 285, formerly OW&WR No 63, was built by Fairbairn's in 1861, being identical to Kirtley's engines for the Midland Railway. It was withdrawn in 1883 — though the Midland engines lasted until the 1920s. *Bucknall Collection/IAL*

double frames, 5ft 3in wheels and 16in + 24in cylinders. The first three were delivered in 1853 and the others in 1855. The other engines were slightly smaller, with 5ft 0in wheels, and were numbered 9 and 11-19 (GWR Nos 259, 269-77), the first two being delivered in January 1857 and the remainder in 1858. Why the last engine of the first class (No 10) had a higher number than the first of the second class — built a year later — is a mystery! None of these engines was rebuilt and they continued working from Hereford and Pontypool until their boilers wore out, whereupon they were scrapped between 1876-1881. Among their duties were the working of coal trains northwards over the Shrewsbury & Hereford Joint Line.

There were only two other six-coupled engines owned by the Company, these being double-framed 0-6-0Ts, with both well and back tanks — described in the Minutes as 'Duck Back Engines' — also built by

40

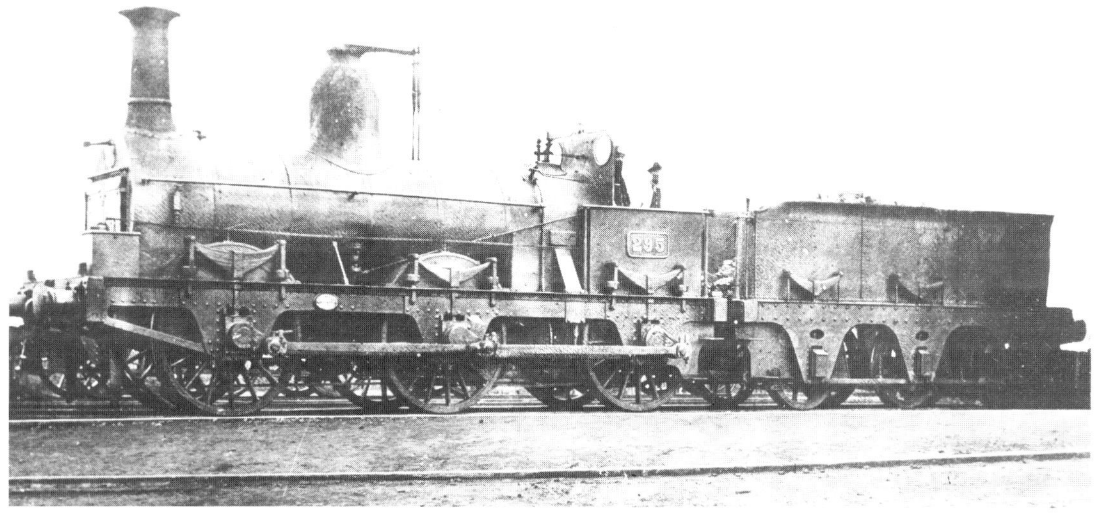

41

**42**
2-2-2 No 211 was built for the WMR by Beyer
Peacock's in 1861. Seen here in original condition, it
was 'renewed' as a 2-4-0 of the '196' class in 1883.
*Bucknall Collection/IAL*

Wilson's in 1856. Nos 7 and 8 (GWR Nos 235 and
236) had 5ft 0in wheels and 18in + 24in cylinders.
Used at first on the Llanhilleth branch, they later
worked as banking engines on heavy coal trains from
Pontypool Road. Both were withdrawn from service in
October 1877.

The first four-coupled passenger engines were three
built by Dodds & Co and purchased by Brassey in
December 1854. Nos 20-22 (GWR Nos 194, 195 and
227) were built as 0-4-2 tender engines with inside
frames, 4ft 6in coupled wheels and 14in + 20in
cylinders, and were fitted with Dodd's wedge motion.
However, by the time they passed into GWR hands,
No 22 had been altered to a side tank — presumably
at Hereford. In December 1865, No 195 was altered
to an 0-4-0 saddle tank and fitted with link motion. Its
fellow, No 194, also received new link motion and
reversing gear, being altered to a saddle tank at the
same time. This was done at Wolverhampton in
August 1872, but in this case the engine remained as
an 0-4-2. Both these engines went to Birkenhead in
their later years, working in the docks; Nos 195 was
withdrawn in 1879, and No 194 lasted about 18
months longer.

No 22 (GWR No 227), already a tank engine, was
sold in March 1870 to the Bishop's Castle Railway
where it was named *Perseverance* — an apt name for
that financially chronically-sick line, though the name
may have been inspired by the vagaries of its Dodd's
wedge motion! Later transferred to the Wrexham,
Mold & Connah's Quay Railway (who shared the
same General Manager and Receiver as the Bishop's
Castle) it ended its days in colliery service in the late
1890s.

There were four passenger engines by Wilson's,
these being 2-4-0s similar to some on the OW&WR.
They carried the numbers 27-30 and were also named
— *Antelope*, *Reindeer*, *Elk* and *Gazelle*. The wheels
were 6ft 0in and cylinders 16in + 22in. They were
twice rebuilt by the GWR (Nos 190-3), the first
rebuilding being between 1872 and 1874, with the
second between 1888 and 1893. At the first rebuilding,
the wheelbase was altered — being lengthened
between the coupled wheels by five inches. Working
mainly from Worcester with the '180' class to
Newport, Didcot and Wolverhampton, and also to
Shrewsbury via the Severn Valley line, they lasted in

**43**
No 211 in rebuilt condition, at Worcester, Shrub Hill. The last survivor of the class, No 211 was withdrawn in 1920 (though two engines found their way back to the GWR when the Cambrian Railways was absorbed in 1922). *LGRP, courtesy David & Charles*

service until the turn of the century, being withdrawn between 1899 and 1903. No 191 was at the Evesham sub-shed in 1901.

**The West Midland Railway**
During its brief existence the WMR placed a number of new engines in service, three of which (Nos 7, 13 and 19) have already been mentioned as 'renewals'. The remainder were numbered 38 (another replacement), 60-70 and 90-114.

The first batch, delivered in 1861-2, consisted of 12 0-6-0s with double frames, built by W. Fairbairn & Son, being of Kirtley's standard MR design — and identical with GWR Nos 280 and 281, these engines being GWR Nos 282-93. Little was done to them and they were all withdrawn between 1882-6 (though some of their contemporaries on the MR survived to become LMS engines, not being withdrawn until the mid-

1920s). They were stationed mainly at Worcester, one of their chief duties being the working of the salt trains to London — on which they were replaced by some of the first 'Dean Goods'.

Also in 1861, two 2-4-0 side tank engines for branch work were delivered by Beyer, Peacock & Co, Nos 68 and 69 (GWR Nos 225 and 226) were of that firm's standard design, having 5ft 0in wheels and 15in + 20in cylinders, being similar to those engines which were well-known on the Isle of Wight (and on the neighbouring East & West Junction Railway at Stratford-on-Avon). Neither was rebuilt and they were withdrawn in 1883 and 1880 respectively — though their Isle of Wight relatives lasted well into the 1920s. No 225 worked on the Stratford-on-Avon branch, while No 226 was employed between Malvern Wells and Worcester, but both spent several years at Hereford.

Next came two classes of passenger engines, also by Beyer, Peacock, the first consisting of six 2-2-2s, Nos 100-5 (GWR Nos 209-14) which were delivered in 1861. With 6ft 6in wheels and 16in + 20in cylinders, they were of Beyer's standard design. They worked for some years over the line between Oxford, Worcester and Wolverhampton, before moving north to Shrewsbury and Chester prior to being completely renewed at Wolverhampton in 1883. The second class, also of six engines were 2-4-0s having many features in common with the previous class. Nos 106-11 (GWR

Nos 196-201) were delivered in 1862, having 6ft 0in coupled wheels and outside bearings for the leading wheels. Nos 196 and 200 were rebuilt with new boilers at Wolverhampton in 1877, when shaped weatherboards with side sheets and 'Wolverhampton' chimneys were fitted. The class worked between Wolverhampton, Worcester, Hereford and Newport, most of them being shedded at Worcester.

Both classes were reconstructed or 'renewed' to become one class of new 2-4-0s, little of the original engines remaining except the outside frames at the leading end! To all intents and purposes they were 'renewals' — a word which could mean anything at Wolverhampton — but some were described as 'rebuilds', others as 'renewals' and yet others as being 'new engines complete'. This reconstruction began in 1879 with No 201, followed by Nos 197 and 199 in 1880-1, these three appearing as 2-4-0Ts (the first

engine having condensers fitted) and were intended as express passenger tank engines. The next engine, No 198 — by then the only one in original condition — was also intended to become a tank engine, but was eventually renewed as a tender engine in October 1882, being followed by the six Singles which were all done in 1883.

The three tank engines were converted to tender engines in 1884-5, and the final two engines (Nos 196 and 200) were reconstructed in 1887, making a uniform class of 12. They had 6ft 2in wheels, 17in + 24in cylinders, and standard Wolverhampton boilers with middle domes and flush firebox casing. They later received a wide range of boilers. Several engines eventually carrying Belpaire boilers, and eight engines had $17\frac{1}{2}$in cylinders.

They were shedded mainly at Wolverhampton and worked all over the former West Midland system, while several later went north to Shrewsbury or Chester. All were withdrawn between 1911 and 1920, except No 209 which was an early withdrawal in 1903. However, Nos 212 and 213 were sold to Mr A. R. Angus to demonstrate his system of automatic train control on the semi-derelict West Somerset Mineral Railway; they were later sold to the Cambrian



**44**

'196' class No 201 was always a 2-4-0, being built by Beyer's in 1862. 'Renewed' in 1879 as seen here, note the early slotted signal. *Real Photos*

Railways and returned to the GWR in 1922, as Nos 1329 and 1328 respectively, being withdrawn in 1926-7.

The last engines built for the WMR were four 0-6-0s which were erected at Worcester in 1862, Nos 38 and 112-4 (GWR Nos 260-3) had 5ft 0in wheels and 16in + 24in cylinders, being similar to the renewals Nos 7, 13 and 19. All bore a strong likeness to the Kirtley engines purchased from the MR and those built by Fairbairn's; and had their frames lengthened as well as receiving new 17in cylinders, but none was rebuilt with new boiler. They remained at Worcester, working with the '280' class on the London salt trains and other duties until withdrawn in 1886-7.

### Shrewsbury & Hereford Railway, and the Tenbury Railway

When the S&HR was leased jointly to the LNWR, GWR and WMR in July 1862, the locomotives were divided — 14 going to the LNWR and 15 to the latter Companies. These became WMR Nos 115-29 and came into GWR stock in 1863.

The passenger engines which came to the GWR were Nos 1-6, built by Vulcan Foundry in 1853-4, these being small 2-2-2s with outside frames, 5ft 6in driving wheels and 15in + 20in cylinders. They became WMR Nos 115-20 (GWR Nos 215-20) and all were withdrawn in 1875-6. The goods engines were of two types; four being 0-4-2 tender engines built by Vulcan Foundry in 1853-4, with 4ft 10in wheels and 15in + 24in cylinders — WMR Nos 122-5 (GWR Nos 202-5) — and all were withdrawn between 1870

**45**
In final condition with Belpaire boiler fitted in 1910, No 201 was withdrawn in 1917. *Real Photos*

and 1875. Four similar engines delivered by Vulcan Foundry in 1855 were 0-6-0s, these being Nos 126-9 in the WMR list (GWR Nos 298-301); two were withdrawn in 1870 and the other two in 1879 — though Nos 229 and 301 were actually sent to Swindon, from Oxford, as early as 1874. There is some doubt as to their original numbers, these eight engines — together with the Tenbury Railway engine — are stated to have been S&HR Nos 10-18 but no details are known.

The Tenbury Railway engine was a Crewe pattern 2-4-0 well tank built by Jones & Son (Liverpool) in March 1856. Allotted WMR No 121, it became GWR No 228 and was withdrawn in 1872.

### The Leominster & Kington Railway

Two Crewe pattern well-tanks, similar to No 228, were inherited from the Leominster & Kington Railway. They were also built by Jones & Son, having 5ft 6in wheels and 14in + 20in cylinders; the only difference from the Tenbury engine being that the latter had 15in cylinders. Both engines were transferred away from their original haunts, as when both were sent to Swindon in 1874, No 229 was at Westbourne Park(!) and No 230 at Oxford. They were withdrawn in 1878.

# 5  Paddington to Worcester, Wolverhampton and Hereford

The main line of the Oxford, Worcester & Wolverhampton Railway was, of course, between those places mentioned in its title, and this continued to be the main line of both the WMR and what became, after 1863, the 'West Midland Section' of the GWR. However, over the years the importance of the service to and from Wolverhampton greatly declined, while that between Paddington and Malvern or Hereford increased. Thus the 1902 Time Tables still gave the principal service as being 'London, Oxford, Evesham, Worcester, Kidderminster, Stourbridge & Wolverhampton', with the Malvern and Hereford trains being shown in the table 'Birmingham, Worcester, Malvern, Hereford, Pontypool Road, Bristol, Cardiff and New Milford' — the latter also contained the important Birmingham and Cardiff through service.

By 1932, the main service was shown as being 'London, Oxford, Evesham, Worcester & Malvern', though full details were given only for the Oxford to Worcester section. Further tables gave the 'London, Worcester, Kidderminster & Wolverhampton' service, full details being given only for the section between Worcester and Wolverhampton. The full service between Worcester and Hereford was still given in those pages devoted to the Birmingham to South Wales service — and Malvern was not even mentioned in the table heading.

A further change had taken place by 1947, with a reversion to the original format, showing the entire service between Oxford, Worcester and Wolverhampton in one table, the description now being 'London, Oxford, Evesham, Worcester, Kidderminster, Stourbridge Junction, Dudley and Wolverhampton' — this being the first mention of the important borough of Dudley! The Malvern and Hereford service now appeared in tables headed 'Worcester, Hereford, Newport, Bristol and Cardiff', there being no mention whatever of Malvern; and although the Birmingham and Cardiff through service continued to be of considerable importance, Birmingham was not shown in the table heading!

The earliest days of the London and Worcester service were, of course concerned not with Paddington, but with Euston, the trains travelling via Bletchley and the LNWR's Buckinghamshire line. Only one train was run each day specially for the Worcester line, the rest of the service being provided by through carriages attached to main line trains. The fastest time between London and Worcester was four hours for the $129\frac{1}{2}$ miles, this being achieved by one train in each direction.

Paddington finally succeeded Euston as the London station for the West Midlands lines in October 1861. Prior to this, the GWR connections to and from Handborough were slightly improved in July and an express in each direction was introduced between Oxford and Worcester. The down train, off the 6.30pm broad gauge Birmingham express from Paddington, reached Worcester at 9.25pm, and was then joined to the 5.00pm through train from Euston to Wolverhampton (LNWR). The up express left Worcester at 7.15am, connected with a Birmingham train at Oxford, and enabled passengers to be in London by 10.30am, which was an hour earlier than had previously been possible. Those trains as long as they lasted — which was not for long — were the only good trains between Paddington and Worcester. The new standard gauge through service inaugurated on 1 October was miserably slow and remained so for nearly 30 years. This was due, in part, to the ingrained conviction that no standard gauge train could ever run as fast as a broad gauge one — and the GWR had no intention of acccelerating their broad gauge services!

In 1880, the best down service consisted of the Worcester portion of the 4.45pm from Paddington, which left Oxford at 6.15pm and consisted of three eight-wheeled carriages (the Wolverhampton portion — known as the 'Zulu' or 'Northern Zulu' had five or

six similar carriages): it was due at Worcester at 7.45pm after four stops.

It was not until 1891, a few months prior to the final abolition of the broad gauge, that any major changes were made and the service to and from Worcester and Malvern somewhat improved. It is significant that it was Malvern which was the beneficiary from such changes as were made. Hereford continued, in Paddington's eyes, to be reached via Gloucester, and there

**46**

Dean 'Bogie Single' No 3069 *Earl of Chester* on up Worcester express near Hayes, c1910.
*Ian Allan Library*

**47**

2-4-0 No 2214 on Worcester line train passing Southall, c1910. '2721' class 0-6-0ST in rear.
*Rixon Bucknall Collection/IAL*

**48**
'Saint' class No 2927 *Saint Patrick* heads a Worcester line train at Tilehurst in the 1920s. *Real Photos*

was little incentive in improving the service beyond Malvern or to Kidderminster. Not until 1900 did Worcester receive further attention, when a new non-stop express each way was introduced in July, the down train taking 2hrs 15min, and the up train 2hrs 20min. Marvellous to relate, this service ran to and from Hereford. Known as the 'Worcester, Malvern and Hereford Corridor Express', the departure time from Paddington was at 1.40pm, with Hereford being reached at 4.55pm: the up train left Hereford at 12.45pm and was due at Paddington at 4.10pm. Though not mentioned in the title, there were also TC to and from Stourbridge. This was the only train on the Worcester line advertised as having corridor carriages.

When the WMR was absorbed into the GWR it brought with it about 30 2-4-0s of various sizes and descriptions, and about a dozen similarly varied 2-2-2s for passenger duties. These continued to work over the West Midlands Section; but they were soon joined by GWR express engines, as it became the practice for engines working between London and Wolverhampton to make one journey via Worcester and the other via Banbury. This was a feature which was to persist throughout the remainder of the 19th century and right up to World War 1. The engines initially involved were the 'Sir Daniel' class 2-2-2s built at Swindon between 1866 and 1869, and these engines continued to be employed on the West Midland line for many years.

By the early 1880s, the Paddington and Wolverhampton service was in charge of larger 2-2-2s, of the '999' or 'Queen' class and of the '157' class. The former were built at Swindon in 1873-5; while the latter dated from 1878-9, when they replaced the original Sharp, Stewart engines with the same numbers built in 1862. Nos 999 Sir Alexander, 1000, 1116, 1121 and 1127 of the former class were shedded at Wolverhampton, as were Nos 157, 160, 161 and 166 of the latter class. The remaining engines of both classes, with the exception of Nos 1122 *Beaconsfield* and 1123 *Salisbury* (which were at Gloucester), were all shedded at Westbourne Park. All these worked some trains in either direction via Worcester until the end of the last century, when they were replaced on the London and Wolverhampton trains by Dean's bogie Singles of the 'Achilles' class and by some of the earlier 4-4-0s.

Worcester still had about a dozen of the original WMR engines which worked one early morning train to Didcot, several turns to Wolverhampton, and others to Hereford and Newport. The greater number of trains between Wolverhampton, Worcester and Oxford or Didcot were worked by the 2-4-0s, Nos

196-201 and 209-14, these being Wolverhampton's 'renewals' of former WMR engines which amounted to a minor standard class. There were also a number of other 2-4-0s at Wolverhampton, among them being Nos 153-6 of the '149' or 'Chancellor' class, which worked to Oxford via Worcester. Towards the end of the last century, the larger, single-framed engines of the '439' class (Nos 439-44) also worked over the West Midland Section: built at Swindon in 1868, they were 'renewed' at Wolverhampton in 1885-6.

The introduction of the 'Corridor Express', non-stop between London and Worcester, brought the first working to Worcester of the beautiful Dean 4-2-2s of the 'Achilles' class, and these engines gradually took over the working of the majority of the principal trains. By 1910, they were almost exclusively in charge of the Oxford and Worcester services (though some larger coupled engines were already making occasional appearances), with engines of the class shedded at both places. For a number of years No 3027 *Worcester* was, most appropriately, shedded at Worcester; others of the class shedded there being Nos 3045 *Hirondelle*, 3050 *Royal Sovereign*, 3056 *Wilkinson* (originally named *Timour*), 3059 *Voltigeur* (renamed *John W. Wilson* in 1908) and 3050 *Warlock* (renamed *John Griffiths* in 1909).

**Paddington, Oxford and Worcester Train Services, 1902**

*Down*

| Paddington (dep) | Oxford (dep) | Stops | Worcester (arr) | Through carriages |
|---|---|---|---|---|
| 9.50am[1] | 11.20am | 3 | 12.47pm | Hereford (2.10pm) Wolverhampton (2.53pm) |
| 1.40pm | 'Corridor Express' | | 3.55pm | Hereford (4.55pm) Stourbridge (5.13pm) |
| 1.45pm | 3.30pm | 3 | 4.40pm | Cheltenham[4] |
| 1.50pm[2] | 3.42pm | All stations | 6.10pm | Wolverhampton (7.43pm) |
| 4.45pm | 6.30pm | 3 | 7.33pm | Wolverhampton (9.13pm) Malvern (8.07pm) |
| 6.50pm[1] | 8.34pm | Principal stations | 10.36pm | Wolverhampton (12.15pm) |

*Up*

| Worcester (dep) | Stops | Oxford (arr) | Paddington (arr) | Through carriages |
|---|---|---|---|---|
| 6.45am | Principal stations | 8.49am[1] SC[2] | 10.25am | Stourbridge (5.55am) |
| 9.12am | 3 | 10.40am SC[2] | 12.00 noon | Wolverhampton (7.20am) Hereford (8.00am)[5] |
| 11.30am | 4 | 1.10pm | 2.33pm | Hereford (9.45am) Cheltenham[4] |
| 1.50pm | 'Corridor Express' | | 4.10pm | Hereford (12.45pm) Stourbridge |
| 2.45pm | 3 | 4.15pm[2, 3] | 5.50pm | Wolverhampton (1.12pm) |
| 5.32pm | 3 | 7.07pm[1, 3] SC | 8.45pm | Wolverhampton (3.45pm) |

SC  Slip Carriage
[1]  Combined with Banbury line train to or from Oxford
[2]  Reading
[3]  Didcot
[4]  via Chipping Norton Junction
[5]  TC conveyed to Forgate Street by Hereford to Birmingham train, then worked round to Shrub Hill

In addition to the through services between Paddington and Hereford via Worcester, there were also three TC services in each direction via Gloucester. Although there was no service on Sundays between Paddington and Hereford via Worcester, the 2.20pm Paddington to Cardiff train had a connection for Hereford at Gloucester. Both of the Hereford to Gloucester trains made connections with trains from New Milford to Paddington: the 10.00am connected with the 6.40pm express (on which refreshments could be obtained!), while the 4.33pm connected with the 10.30am — hardly an express as it only omitted calling at two stations between New Milford and Swindon!

On Sundays there were only two trains between

49

50

51

French Compound Atlantic No 102 *La France* at Moreton-in-Marsh on a Paddington to Worcester train, 7 August 1923. All three Atlantics spent their last years working from Oxford shed.
*H. G. W. Household*



No 3446 *Goldfinch* stands in Moreton-on-Marsh on a Worcester to Paddington express 24 April 1923. 'Bulldogs' handled a wide variety of duties on the West Midland Section for many years.
*H. G. W. Household*



Worcester to Paddington Restaurant Car Express at Camden, headed by No 3715 *City of Hereford* 11 July 1925. By this date, the majority of main line carriages had been repainted in the familiar chocolate and cream livery after a period of 20 years of overall red-brown.
*H. G. W. Household*

Oxford and Worcester, both of which called at all stations. The 7.40am had no connection from Paddington (unless passengers spent the night at Oxford!); but the 5.40pm connected with the 3.20pm. Paddington to Shrewsbury service, arriving at Worcester at 7.50pm and at Wolverhampton at 10.05pm. There was a connection from Worcester to Malvern. The up service also had two trains, calling at every station between Wolverhampton and Oxford. The 8.15am from Wolverhampton left Worcester at 10.15am, arriving at Oxford at 12.25pm where it connected with the 6.50am from Shrewsbury which arrived at Paddington at 2.20pm. Malvern passengers had a connection to Worcester. The second train left Wolverhampton at 3.30pm and Worcester at 5.30pm, there being a connection for Malvern Wells, and arrived at Oxford at 7.40pm; leaving at 8.10pm on the 5.50pm from Wolverhampton via Banbury, Paddington was reached at 9.42pm.

In 1904 the Paddington to Worcester non-stop service was altered to provide a later afternoon departure from Paddington at 4.45pm (the same time as the 'crack' express in 1880), with arrival at Worcester at 7.00pm. Hereford passengers could change at Foregate Street into a new Birmingham to Cardiff express. Previously the last Paddington to Hereford train had been the 1.50pm. The up train now left Worcester at 8.55am and was due at Paddington at 11.10am thus taking five minutes less than the original 'Corridor Express'. Apart from the greater convenience for passengers — allowing a few hours in

London for busines purposes — the new timings allowed for both services to be run using the same set of carriages.

In 1905, the 4.45pm from Paddington, non-stop to Worcester, arrived there at 6.55pm, at Malvern at 7.35pm and at Hereford at 8.30pm. There was also a 6.15pm Dining Car Train which stopped at Reading, Oxford and Evesham, reaching Worcester at 8.47pm. The former 4.45pm now left 10 minutes later, at 4.55pm, and made the usual three stops between Oxford and Worcester. There was now an early morning through train from Malvern (dep 8.20am) and a 12.05pm train from Worcester which stopped only at Oxford (arr 1.15pm) and arrived at Paddington at 2.33pm. The following year the early morning train was extended to commence from Hereford (dep 7.45am) while in 1907 the 6.50pm from Paddington was re-timed to leave at 7.30pm, thus giving a much later evening departure.

A few years later, the opening of the direct route from London to Birmingham via Bicester saw the withdrawal of the principal express service from the old route via Oxford (though some trains continued to be routed that way until the last days of the GWR). This left the important city of Oxford largely dependent on the West Midland services, as a result of which non-stop running from Paddington to Worcester came to an end for a while; though there were one or two trains in later years which ran non-stop to and from Worcester, with one or two others stopping only at Kingham (as Chipping Norton Junction had become). In general, the service did not improve for many years and in many ways the 'palmiest' days were those before World War 1.

In 1914, there were two non-stop Paddington to Worcester trains, the 4.45pm (arriving at 6.55pm) and the 1.40pm which took five minutes longer (arriving at 3.55pm). Five other trains took between 2hr 51min and 3hr 10min. By 1918, there were only five down and six up trains, most of these serving all stations between Oxford and Worcester. In July 1920, non-stop running was restored between London and Worcester, with the 1.30pm; while the 8.55am from Worcester gave a fast morning service, arriving at Paddington at 11.15am after stopping only at Oxford.

The GWR introduced Standard Departure Times in 1924, departures from Paddington for the West Midland line being at 9.45pm, 12.45pm, 4.45pm and 7.45pm, with additional trains at 8.40pm and 6.05pm. The former 1.30pm 'non-stop' now became the 12.45pm, still non-stop, but with SC for Kingham and Evesham — the former consisting of two or three TC for Cheltenham.

The 'Achilles' class of bogie Singles was gradually withdrawn from service and all had gone by 1915. From about 1912 the double-framed 4-4-0s of the

'Flower' class (by then including also the 'Badmintons' and 'Atbaras') were used on the Paddington and Worcester services: three of them being shedded at Worcester, while others were at Oxford. For a period, the famous 'Cities' were also used on these trains, and one or two of them — including No 3700 *Durban* — were shedded at Worcester, others being at Oxford. As on many other main lines, they were followed by the outside cylinder 'Counties' as the principal express passenger engines, but their reign in this role was brief and they had largely been replaced by 1923. Some were shedded at Hereford and Oxford during the 1920s: from the latter shed they covered all the main line duties until the advent of the 'Halls' — though one or two 'Saints' were there in the mid-1920s. Some unusual workings took place during World War 1, when 'Barnum' class 2-4-0s, several of which were

shedded at Oxford, were used in emergencies on heavy expresses between Paddington and Worcester.

The three De Glehn Compound Atlantics, Nos 102 *La France*, 103 *President* and 104 *Alliance*, originally used on the West of England main line, had moved to the Wolverhampton and Worcester expresses between 1907 and 1913. They were then sent to Oxford and used on less-important duties to Paddington and Birmingham; however, they still worked to Worcester on occasions, and No 102 was photographed at Moreton-in-Marsh on a Paddington to Worcester express in August 1923. The next class to appear were the 'Saints', some engines from Wolverhampton appearing on Paddington to Worcester expresses as early as 1910-1, and in 1923 four of the class were at Worcester. Their period of regular service came to an end when the four-cylinder 'Stars' began to appear on these duties in 1927, and by 1932 there were none shedded at Worcester; though by then they had begun to be allocated to Hereford — a shed which was later to become famous for its collection of those vintage engines. The 'Stars' had been used on the Worcester line on occasions some years prior to 1927, but their regular employment dated from that year; by 1932, there were seven of the class shedded at Worcester.

**52**
The pride of Worcester shed, where it was shedded for most of its life, 'Castle' class No 5063 *Earl Baldwin* is in charge of the 6.45pm Paddington to Malvern express, passing Sonning Box.  *M. W. Earley*

*Down*

| Paddington (dep) | Oxford (dep) | Stops | Worcester (arr) | Through caerriages |
|---|---|---|---|---|
| 9.45am[2] | 11.15am | Principal stations | 12.38pm | Wolverhampton (2.11pm) Hereford (2.15pm) |
| 12.45pm | RC | Kingham | 2.55pm | Cheltenham[4] Hereford (3.54pm) Stourbridge (3.49pm) |
| 1.45pm[2] RC | 3.10pm | 6 | 4.37pm | Malvern (5.00pm) Stourbridge (5.35pm) |
| 4.45pm RC | 6.00pm | Moreton-in-Marsh, Evesham | 7.08pm | Hereford (8.30pm) Stourbridge (8.01pm) |
| 6.05pm RC[2] | 7.30pm | 5 | 8.50pm | Malvern (9.15pm) |
| 7.40pm X[2] | 9.10pm | Principal stations | 11.00pm | — |

*Up*

| Worcester (dep) | Stops | Oxford (arr) | Paddington (arr) | Through carriages |
|---|---|---|---|---|
| 6.35am | Principal stations | 8.30am | 9.50am | — |
| 8.55am | Evesham, Moreton-in-Marsh | 10.05am | 11.15am | Wolverhampton (7.00am) Hereford (dep 7.25am) |
| 12.10pm RC | 5 | 1.30pm[2] SC | 3.00pm | — |
| 2.00pm RC | Evesham | 3.10pm | 4.20pm | Hereford (12.50pm) Kidderminster (1.20pm) |
| 6.10pm RC | Evesham, Moreton-in-Marsh, Kingham | 7.35pm[1,2,3] | 9.20pm | Hereford (4.55pm) |

RC  Restaurant Car
SC  Slip Carriage
[1]  Combined with Banbury line train from Oxford
[2]  Reading
[3]  Ealing Broadway
[4]  via Kingham

There were two trains in each direction on Sundays. The 10.10am from Paddington (RC) called at Reading, Oxford (dep 11.55am) and all stations open on Sundays, arriving at Worcester at 1.45pm. TC for Hereford (arr 2.57pm). The 4.10pm called at Ealing Broadway, Reading, Oxford (dep 5.50pm) and then repeated the performance of the 10.10am, arriving at Worcester at 7.55pm.

The up service consisted of the 10.25am and 6.15pm trains from Worcester, both of which stopped at all stations between Worcester and Oxford which were open on Sunday. The former arrived at Oxford at 12.40pm and was combined with the 8.55am from Shrewsbury, calling at Didcot and Reading, to reach Paddington at 2.40pm. The 6.10pm had TC from Hereford (dep 5.00pm) and RC; arriving at Oxford at 8.12pm, it then stopped only at Reading and reached Paddington at 9.40pm.

Although the 'Stars' continued to be used on some of the more important duties, there being three at Oxford in 1938 — Nos 4004 *Morning Star*, 4021 *The British Monarch* and 4052 *Princess Beatrice* — while there were still two at Worcester, Nos 4040 *Princess Maud* and 4051 *Princess Helena*, their successors, the famous 'Castles' had taken over the principal role by the mid-1930s. In 1938 there were four shedded at Worcester, Nos 5042 *Winchester Castle*, 5049 *Earl of Plymouth*, 5050 *Earl of St Germans* and 5063 *Earl Baldwin*; the latter engine was always maintained in the most immaculate condition as the 'flagship' of the local fleet — for Stanley Baldwin was a Worcestershire man! — though all Worcester's express passenger engines were always well-maintained and clean, even during the war years. By the following year, No 5042 had moved to Gloucester in exchange for No 4086 *Builth Castle*, the engine responsible for the first 100mph recorded for a 'Castle' and the first for any GWR engine since *City of Truro* back in 1904: this was down Honeybourne bank with the 12.45pm Paddington to Hereford express.

A number of 'Halls' gradually collected at Worcester and Hereford, there being five at each shed by 1938, when Hereford also had two 'Saints' Nos 2921 *Saint Dunstan* and 2980 *Coeur de Lion*; while there were no less than 10 'Halls' at Oxford. Some of the less-important Paddington trains were sometimes in charge of a 'Hall'.

In the summer of 1935 a diesel railcar service between Oxford and Hereford was introduced, with connection to and from Paddington at Oxford. The down service left Oxford at 10.20am and the up departure from Hereford was at 2.05pm. In July 1937 the fastest scheduled time ever for the Paddington to Hereford was introduced, when the 12.45pm from Paddington was allowed 3hr 4min, including the Oxford, Worcester and Malvern stops. However, the time of 2hr 10min, between Paddington and Worcester had been in force as long ago as 1903, though that had been for a non-stop run. The 4.45pm made additional stops at Moreton-in-Marsh and Evesham, reaching Worcester in 2hr 21min, at 7.06pm. The fastest up

**53**

Prior to the advent of the 'Castles', the 'Stars' were the premier express passenger engines. Relegated to less-exacting duties in its latter years, No 4007 *Swallowfield Park* (of Worcester shed) stands in Hereford station in 1951, shortly before being withdrawn from service.   *C. R. L. Coles*

**54**

Nos 6985 *Parwick Hall* and 2937 *Clevedon Court* head the 4.48pm Hereford to Paddington in the golden summer of 1952. Hereford provided both engines for this working, one returning from Worcester on the 4.45pm ex-Paddington and the other on a fruit special. Combinations of a 'Saint' and 'Star' and double-headed 'Saints' could be seen on occasions.
*R. J. Doran*

service was that leaving Worcester at 8.55am, which stopped at the same stations as the 4.45pm down and reached London at 10.10am, a time of 2hr 15min.

The war years saw a general deterioration of train services, and the Paddington to Worcester line was no exception. In the final Time Tables issued by the GWR for the winter of 1947, the fastest time between London and Worcester was no less than 2hr 40min, for the down service and 2hr 35min by the up service. These were by the 4.45pm and 8.55am respectively — both trains inheriting the tradition of being the fastest service of the day over the West Midland Section, which had been maintained since the beginning of this century.

**Paddington, Oxford and Worcester Train Services, Winter 1947**

*Down*

| Paddington (dep) | Oxford (dep) | Stops | Worcester (arr) | Through carriages |
|---|---|---|---|---|
| 9.45am[2, 3] | 11.28am | 4 | 12.55pm | Hereford (2.20pm) |
| 1.45pm[2, 3] | 3.20pm | 5 | 4.49pm | Stourbridge (5.52pm) |
| 4.45pm BC | 6.08pm | Moreton-in-Marsh Evesham | 7.25pm | Hereford (8.40pm) Wolverhampton (9.28pm) |
| 6.05pm[2] RC | 7.40pm | Principal stations | 9.22pm | Malvern (9.49pm) |
| Also | | | | |
| 4.40pm[2] | 6.24pm | All except 3 | 8.34pm | Worcester |

*Up*

| Worcester (dep) | Stops | Oxford (arr) | Paddington (arr) | Through carriages |
|---|---|---|---|---|
| 6.35pm | Most stations | 8.32am | 10.00am | — |
| 8.55pm BC | Evesham, Moreton-in-Marsh | 10.10am | 11.30am | Hereford (7.45pm) Wolverhampton (6.50am) |
| 12.15pm RC | Principal stations | 1.57pm[2] | 3.35pm | Hereford (10.48am) |
| 2.10pm | Evesham, Moreton-in-Marsh, Kingham | 3.30pm | 5.05pm | Hereford (12.47pm) Wolverhampton (12.05pm) |
| 6.05pm RC | 4 | 7.30pm | 9.05pm | — |

*Sundays Down*

| Paddington (dep) | Oxford | Stops | Worcester | Through carriages |
|---|---|---|---|---|
| 10.10am[1, 2] RC | 11.55 | 4 | 1.25pm | Hereford RC (2.51pm) |
| 4.00pm[1, 2] | 5.50pm | 13 | 8.05pm | Wolverhampton (9.58pm) |
| 6.20pm[2] | 7.50pm | Moreton-in-Marsh, Evesham, Pershore | 9.15pm | Hereford (10.22pm) |

(This gave Hereford a later service via Worcester on Sundays than on weekdays — when last departure via Worcester was at 4.45pm. There was, however, a 6.35pm service via Gloucester).

*Sundays Up*

| Worcester (dep) | Stops | Oxford (arr) | Paddington (arr) | Through carriages |
|---|---|---|---|---|
| 11.45am | Evesham, Honeybourne, Moreton-in-Marsh | 1.10pm[2] | 2.55pm | Hereford (10.35am) |
| 6.05pm | 13 | 8.05pm[2] | 9.50pm | |
| 6.47pm RC | 5 | 8.22pm | 10.00pm | Hereford RC (5.30pm) |

BC  Buffet Car
RC  Restaurant Car
[1]  Combined with Banbury line train
[2]  Calls at Reading
[3]  Calls at Didcot

By 1947 there were six 'Castles' at Worcester; Nos 4086 *Builth Castle,* 4092 *Dunraven Castle,* 5017 *St Donat's Castle,* 5063 *Earl Baldwin* — which spent all its life, except the last year of so, working from Worcester — 5092 *Tresco Abbey* and 7005 *Lamphey Castle,* the latter being one of 10 postwar 'Castles' built by the GWR in 1946 (and later re-named *Sir Edward Elgar* after another Worcestershire man). There was also now one 'Castle' at Hereford, this being none other than the celebrated No 4079 *Pendennis Castle,* which had taken part in the locomotive exchange with the LNER in 1925. Strangely enough, Hereford does not appear ever to have had any 'Stars'. However, there were still two of the latter class at Worcester, Nos 4007 *Swallowfield Park* (formerly at Gloucester) and 4051 *Princess Helena,* while there were four at Oxford; Nos 4004 *Morning Star,* 4021 *The British Monarch* and 4052 *Princess Beatrice* having been joined by No 4049 *Princess Maud* from Worcester.

Both 'Stars' and 'Halls' were employed from time to time on trains to and from Paddington, Oxford and Worcester each having about a dozen of the latter class. Hereford's prewar allocation of five 'Halls' had been reduced to three, no doubt because of the large number of 'Saints' which had been transferred there during the war years. There were no less than eight of the grand old engines; Nos 2920 *Saint David* (ex-Chester), 2924 *Saint Helena* (ex-Leamington), 2932 *Ashton Court* (another engine formerly at Chester), 2937 *Clevedon Court* (ex-Reading), 2944 *Highnam Court* (exchanged with Gloucester for No 2980 *Coeur de Lion*), 2948 *Stackpole Court* (ex-Newport) and 2987 *Bride of Lammermoor* (ex-Cardiff). Hereford's other prewar 'Saint', No 2921 *Saint Dunstan* had been withdrawn in 1945.

Although Hereford's 'Saints' worked regularly over the West to North route to Shrewsbury and down to Newport, they were also often employed on the through trains to Birmingham and on Hereford and Paddington through carriages to and from Worcester, where it was sometimes possible to see both *Saint Helena* and *Princess Helena* at Shrub Hill station at the same time.

**55**

Most appropriately, No 3027 *Worcester* was shedded at Worcester for many years and was used on the most important express passenger duties. Seen here as rebuilt with a Standard No 2 Boiler, No 3027 was withdrawn in 1914. *Ian Allan Library*

55

# 6 All stations to Worcester — local services on the main lines

Although the through trains to and from London, together with the cross-country service between Birmingham and Cardiff, were always regarded as the most important passenger services on the West Midland lines, the many local trains — most of which stopped at all stations — had an even greater importance as far as the pattern of life in the numerous small towns and villages was concerned. With the advent of the railway, even though it was the 'Old Worse and Worse', it was possible for the inhabitants of Adlestrop and Campden (for some reason neither the OW&WR or the GWR ever acknowledged that it was Chipping Campden), Fladbury and Pershore, Hartlebury and numerous other places, to 'go up' to Worcester with comparative ease. It was the railway which also made possible the development of Droitwich and Malvern as select inland resorts and spa towns, as well as the beginnings of the migration to the country of the well-to-do professional and business families which was to give even a provincial city such as Worcester its daily commutors.

The importance which the GWR attached to the residential traffic to and from Malvern can be judged by comparing the service enjoyed by that place with that endured by Hereford. In the early 1860s there were nine trains in each direction between Worcester and Malvern, whereas the Worcester and Hereford service was a mere four trains, as was that on the Oxford to Worcester section of the main line.

Over the years the local services on all sections of the main lines grew very considerably, though the least growth was to be found on the Oxford to Worcester section: ironically, this was the only section of the former OW&WR which Brunel considered could ever be profitable! This was especially true of the line north of Worcester, where the expansion of Birmingham and Wolverhampton created a fairly intensive suburban service to Stourbridge and Kidderminster. Even between Worcester and Honeybourne, with the crea-tion of a through route beyond Stratford-on-Avon to Leamington and Birmingham, there was a noticeable growth in train services and traffic.

In 1902, there were no trains on weekdays between Oxford and Worcester apart from those to and from Paddington, with the exception of the 4.35pm from Reading which stopped at every station to Worcester (arr 8.55pm). Between Chipping Norton Junction and Oxford there was one return working. From Worcester there was a 5.15am train to Moreton-in-the-Marsh, which called at Pershore, Evesham, Campden and Blockley — in each case 'to set down Passengers from Worcester and beyond' (though there was no train arriving at Worcester from anywhere on the GWR until 6.15am). This was a train which was to become an institution, and it was still to be found in the Time Tables — and with the same note — down to the last days of the GWR, although running an hour earlier in later years. In 1902 it return from Moreton at 7.40am and called at all stations to Wolverhampton: by 1932 it left at 7.30am and ran to Hereford; while in 1947 it terminated at Foregate Street.

By 1932, there were three stopping trains in each direction between Oxford and Worcester, most of which connected at Oxford with trains to or from Paddington. There were still three such trains in 1947, though they now included a morning working by a diesel railcar from Malvern to Oxford and then back to Worcester (which spent 40min at Moreton-in-the-Marsh on the outward journey) and a return working by an auto-train which left Oxford at 2.10pm and did not arrive back there until 9.25pm. Between Oxford and Kingham there were a handful of trains by 1932 — one in each direction on Saturdays being between Oxford and Cheltenham (though not a return working, as both trains departed at almost the same time). In 1947, the service had increased a little, being shared by auto-trains and diesel railcars.

The 1932 Time Tables included an 8.30am train

from Moreton which only went as far as Campden; returned from there at 9.10am to terminate at Moreton — and disappeared from the tables! Neither engine or carriages appeared to be used for any other train! Moreton was for many years served by a late afternoon train from Cheltenham, which reversed at Honeybourne, and later returned to Cheltenham, again reversing at Honeybourne! The Cheltenham crew cannot have been very pleased at the uncoupling and coupling-up which was involved. However, this provided connections with the up Dining Car Train from Worcester (dep 6.10pm in 1932; dep 6.50pm in 1947) and from the 4.45pm from Paddington, both of which stopped at Moreton but not at Honeybourne.

The section between Worcester and Honeybourne was much better served, largely thanks to the through trains to and from Stratford-on-Avon and beyond. In 1902, three trains to Worcester came through from Stratford or beyond: the 7.40am from Leamington continued past Worcester to Hartlebury and thence to Shrewsbury via the Severn Valley line; while the 5.55pm from Birmingham arrived at Worcester at 8.00pm. In the reverse direction, the 7.30am from Worcester continued to Birmingham and eventually terminated at Shrewsbury at 11.45am; while the 4.50pm continued beyond Stratford to Leamington and ended its journey at Oxford at 8.57pm. There was several trains in each direction between Worcester and Stratford or Leamington, also a late evening train from Worcester to Evesham — which formed the 9.05am from Evesham to Leamington, the engine and carriages remaining at Evesham overnight.

By 1932, except on Saturdays there was a 7.05am train from Evesham to Pershore, which returned as the

**56**
'Bulldog' No 3385 *Newport* on a down stopping train at Campden, 11 July 1925. *H. G. W. Household*

**57**
One of the 'Bulldogs' with combined name and number plates, No 3345 *Smeaton* on a stopping train at Worcester, Shrub Hill, in 1928. No 3345 was withdrawn in 1936. *J. A. G. H. Coltas*

7.35am through train to Birmingham (Snow Hill): this was an indication of the way in which a small town such as Pershore now had commutor traffic for Birmingham. However, in 1947 Pershore commutors had to leave at 6.48am (on the 6.35am from Worcester) and change at Evesham, there being trains from Evesham at 7.05am for Leamington and at 8.00am for Birmingham.

The morning Worcester to Birmingham train and the evening return working continued right down to 1947; though by 1932 it was leaving Worcester at 8.10am and running to Moor Street, the return working remained unchanged at 5.55pm Snow Hill even in 1947. Diesel railcars shared in the service between Worcester and Honeybourne with some running to and from Stratford. The through service between Leamington and Worcester had dwindled to one train in 1947, this being the 4.20pm from Leamington — which was also the only train to continue beyond Worcester, terminating at Wolverhampton at 8.12pm. Finally, there was a daily

morning trip from Honeybourne to Evesham and back by an auto-train, this being the one which ran between Cheltenham and Honeybourne.

The Sunday service in 1902 consisted of the two trains in each direction between Oxford and Worcester. By 1932, south of Honeybourne there were still only the two down and three up Paddington trains; though there were three or four trains between Worcester and Evesham, also a return working between Honeybourne and Evesham by the Cheltenham auto-train. There was also an early morning train from Birmingham (dep 7.05am to Worcester, with a return working leaving Worcester at 6.40pm. There was little change in 1947, when there were still only two stopping trains each way between Oxford and Worcester: however, by this time a number of country stations were closed on Sundays. The only other trains were a return working of an auto-train between Cheltenham and Worcester, arriving at Worcester at 11.30am and leaving again at 1.05pm and a late evening auto-train from Worcester to Evesham and back.

North of Worcester there was considerably more growth over the years, not least in the service between Kidderminster and Birmingham and that between Stourbridge Junction and Wolverhampton. In 1902, in addition to those trains between Worcester and Wolverhampton which formed part of the through services to and from London (most of which stopped at all stations), there were five local trains from Worcester and three from Wolverhampton. There were a few trains between Worcester and Hartlebury in each direction in connection with the Severn Valley line. There was a 7.00am through train from Worcester to Birmingham — which also had through carriages for Wolverhampton — but no less than three through trains from Birmingham to Worcester. Of the latter, the 4.25pm included a TC for Woofferton (detached at Kidderminster); though there was no return working, there was a TC for Wolverhampton leaving Woofferton at 7.07am. There were also a couple of Worcester to Birmingham train which ran via Dudley and Old Hill.

The most important train north of Worcester was that which left Shrub Hill at 9.55am; calling only at the principal stations to Wolverhampton and conveying TC to Manchester (London Road) via Wellington and Crewe. The return working consisted of TC attached to the only Wolverhampton to Hereford through train, leaving Low Level at 3.45pm and which arrived at Foregate Street at 5.05pm. Foregate Street was also served by the through trains in each direction between Cardiff and Birmingham. There were also a few local trains between Kidderminster and either Birmingham or Wolverhampton, and between Stourbridge Junction and Wolverhampton.

Finally, there was a delightful and leisurely train which left Wolverhampton at 4.00pm to call at all stations to Hartlebury where it arrived at 5.15pm. Both crew and train then rested from their labours until 9.30pm, when they returned to Wolverhampton via Bewdley.

By 1932, there were no less than three early morning trains from Worcester to Birmingham, though only one of these was from Shrub Hill (dep 6.38am). The others, from Foregate Street, were provided by the 7.24pm from Colwall and the 8.25am from Malvern: thus had Birmingham's commuter service grown! In each instance there was a return evening working; though the Colwall train terminated at Ledbury. There were also the through trains between Birmingham and Cardiff or Hereford: by 1947, there were no less than eight of these in each direction.

The former Worcester to Manchester through service had been reduced to a through service to Crewe, leaving Worcester at 9.42am in 1932, and there was no return working: by 1947, even the Worcester to Crewe through train had ceased to run. The 9.42am was the first through train to Wolverhampton in 1932, there being five trains in each direction. In 1947, this had been reduced to four trains from Worcester, but increased to seven from Wolverhampton!

Although the early morning train from Worcester to Shrewsbury, via the Severn Valley line, continued to run until 1947, by 1932 this was the only through train in either direction. However, Wolverhampton now provided a train at 10.45am which called at all stations to Hartlebury and then ran over the Severn Valley line to Shrewsbury.

On Sundays, the service in 1902 was little better than that between Worcester and Oxford. Apart from three trains in each direction between Worcester and Wolverhampton, there were one or two between either Birmingham or Wolverhampton and Kidderminster. There was also a Wolverhampton to Hartlebury return working; though this only managed to spend three and a half hours at Hartlebury. By 1932, there had been a considerable change; though there were still only three

**58**
'Metro' 2-4-0T No 1459 and auto-train stand in Worcester, Shrub Hill, in 1928, Built in 1882, No 1459 was withdrawn in 1936, two months after No 3345. *J. A. G. H. Coltas*

**59**
'Bulldog' No 3444 *Cormorant*, of the final 'Bird' series with deeper frames, leaving Stourbridge Junction on a Worcester to Birmingham train.
*Bucknall Collection/IAL*

58

59

Inside-cylinder 2-6-2 No 3920 leaving Stourbridge Junction on a fast train for Birmingham. Rebuilt in 1910 from 'Dean Goods' No 2502, No 3920 was withdrawn in 1932.
*LGRP, courtesy David & Charles*

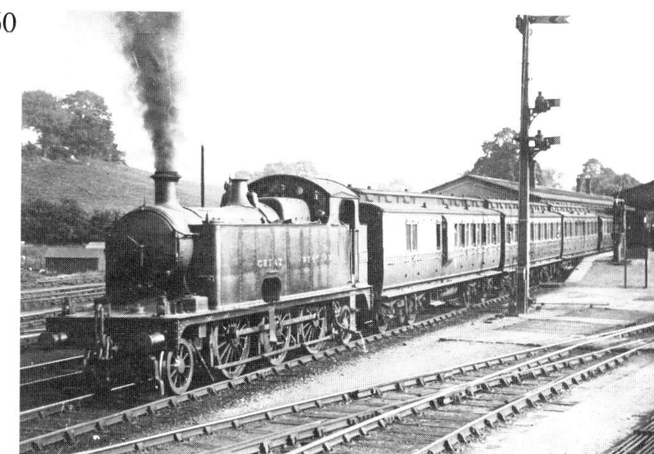

trains each way between Worcester and Wolverhampton. In 1947, although there were still three trains from Worcester, there was only one through train from Wolverhampton — and this was not until 8.25pm.

In 1932, three trains ran during the morning from Birmingham to Malvern or Hereford, with return workings in the evening. However, it was not possible to reach Birmingham from Worcester (by the GWR) until 1.05pm — and then only by waiting for 40min at Stourbridge Junction. Apart from a number of trains north of Kidderminster in each direction, there were only two trains from Birmingham to Hartlebury; the morning train returned to Wolverhampton and the afternoon one returned to Birmingham, both being via Bewdley. In 1947 there was no Shrub Hill to Birmingham through service on Sundays; though there was a train from Snow Hill (dep 4.00pm) to Worcester, as well as two in each direction on the Birmingham and Cardiff service which called at Foregate Street.

In 1902, there were six trains in each direction between Worcester and Hereford, with another five each way between Worcester and Malvern, and three in each direction between Worcester and Gloucester via Ledbury. There was also the 'Corridor Express' and five trains each way between Birmingham and Hereford, four of these being to or from Cardiff. All four of the Birmingham to Cardiff trains had TC for Ross-on-Wye, while two of the Cardiff trains had TC from Ross-on-Wye to Birmingham. The first train from Malvern was at 8.15am from Malvern Wells (where an engine was shedded overnight) and the last was at 10.00pm from Malvern (Great). The first train from Worcester was the 7.35am to Hereford, while the last terminated at Malvern at 11.13pm.

Although by 1932 the service between Worcester and Hereford was but little changed, there had been a considerable increase in the Worcester and Malvern service. There were no longer any through trains between Worcester and Gloucester, though some trains ran to or from Ledbury or Colwall. A considerable number were shown as being by 'Rail Motor Car, one class only' — these being auto-trains. Rather surprisingly, the use of steam railcars does not appear to have been tried on these services, their only local use being between Honeybourne and Evesham or Stratford-on-Avon. The first morning train leaving Worcester at 7.15am was still for Hereford, while the last evening train was an auto-train to Malvern at 10.10pm. Several auto-trains ran to and from Foregate Street. On Thursdays and Saturdays there was a late evening train to Ledbury at 11.00pm, a service which still existed in 1947.

Birmingham was the destination of an early morning train from both Colwall and Malvern, with return workings in the evening. One of the latter ran to Ledbury and then returned to Worcester, but the other train remained overnight at Malvern — despite the engine shed having been closed in 1922. In 1947, there were only five trains from Worcester to Hereford, two having TC from Paddington; though there were also three Birmingham to Cardiff trains, three to Hereford and one to Malvern, all using Foregate Street. There was a similar service in the reverse direction. The service between Worcester and Malvern consisted of about a dozen trains, only a little better than in 1902 and roughly the same as the service on Sundays in 1932! Some of these workings were now by diesel railcar.

In 1902, the service on Sundays consisted of one train in each direction between Worcester and Hereford (at 10.25am from Hereford and at 6.15pm from Worcester) and four each way between Worcester and Malvern. There was still only one stopping train each way between Worcester and Hereford in 1932, though there were now two trains between Birmingham and Hereford as well as an up and down service between Hereford and Paddington. Twelve trains ran between Worcester and Malvern, with another two between Birmingham and Malvern. In 1947, the only trains between Worcester and Hereford were those on the London or Birmingham services; while there were six each way between Worcester and Malvern — four of these being auto-trains.

The original WMR engines continued in charge of

local services until their gradual demise — thus Evesham still had ex-NA&HR 2-4-0 No 191 shedded there in 1901. Their place was taken by GWR engines, often of considerable antiquity; as when there was an influx of the Wolverhampton-built 2-4-0s of the '111' class (which dated from the 1860s) towards the end of the century. Nos 114, 374, 376, 377 and 1007 were at Hereford, and were later joined by No 1010, while Nos 111 and 1003 were also in the area. In later years, No 113 was at Oxford and worked over the West Midland lines. The 'modern' edition of this class, consisting of six engines built in 1889, were also on these duties; Nos 3226-9 being at Worcester or Hereford until about 1907. In the 1890s, several of the 'Sir Daniel' class 2-2-2s, displaced from main line services, were at Oxford and employed on secondary duties which included some turns to Worcester: these were Nos 380 (formerly *North Star*), 382, 387, 471 *Sir Watkin*, 474, 480 and 580.

At the same time, the '481 class renewals were transferred to Worcester and Hereford for secondary duties. The later 2-4-0s of the '806' and '2201' classes were also employed; Nos 806, 807, 810 and 821, which were shedded at Stafford Road, worked over the West Midland line after their use on the Chester expresses had ended, while No 2205 was at Hereford by 1899. Back in the 1870s, Hereford had two of the most unusual engines on the GWR, 2-4-0s Nos 320 and 321 which had been rebuilt at Wolverhampton from condensing tank engines built for working on the underground lines of the Metropolitan Railway. They had outside cylinders, being the only standard gauge engines built by the GW in the 19th century with this feature. Both were withdrawn in 1881. Hereford also had one or two of the '149' class in their later years, and No 56 of the '717' class (for many years the only passenger tender engines at Bordesley shed) was at Worcester from 1902-6. Several other engines of this class also worked from Worcester on occasions.

The 0-4-4Ts of the '3521' class, notorious for their record of derailments in the West of England, found some employment in the area in the late 1890's; No 3547 was at Malvern Wells sub-shed in 1901. The vast majority of passenger tank engines, however, consisted of the little Wolverhampton-built 0-4-2Ts of the '517' class. These worked from Leamington and Birmingham to Worcester, and from Worcester to Malvern, Kidderminster and Stourbridge. There was a noticeable absence of the Swindon-built engines of the 'Metro' class, the only appearance of these engines being that of one or two which worked through to Hereford or Worcester on trains from Cardiff.

Most of the '481' class engines had been withdrawn by 1914, but the '806' and '2201' classes lasted a little longer. A number of these worked around Worcester on local duties, and No 2218 which was withdrawn in

**61**
'517' class 0-4-2T No 1477 heads a train of four-wheeled carriages bound for Kidderminster, seen here near Stourbridge Junction. Built in 1884, No 1477 was withdrawn in December 1937.
*LGRP, courtesy David & Charles*

**62**
'3521' class 4-4-0 No 3531 at Stourbridge Junction on a Wolverhampton to Hartlebury train. Built in 1887 as an 0-4-2T and altered to 0-4-4T in 1891, No 3531 was rebuilt as a tender engine in 1901; superheated in 1911, it was withdrawn in 1927.
*LGRP, courtesy David & Charles*

1921 was among the last survivors of the class. A few of the double-framed engines of the '3201' or 'Stella' class were at Stourbridge by 1915 — that shed being for many years a last home for aged engines! Also there were one or two of the celebrated 'Barnums' (the '3206' class), No 3214 being withdrawn from there in 1931. Some of the 'River' class 2-4-0s, which had all worked from Oxford on secondary trains during the first few years after the reconstruction in 1895-7, were to be found on local work from Worcester during the years just before World War 1 — No 76 *Wye* being withdrawn from Worcester in May 1914.

As the old 2-4-0s were withdrawn, their place was taken by the 'Bulldog' 4-4-0s, Hereford having a large number of them at one time — though they were to be found throughout the West Midland Section. From 1910 there was an exodus from the West of England of the '3521' class 4-4-0s (rebuilt in 1899-1902 from 0-4-4Ts), 14 of which carried domeless boilers, and a positive 'invasion' by these engines of the Worcester Division. They worked both branch and local traffic; even Kidderminster had one of the class, No 3535, in 1926, though that shed had no turntable. As well as working between Gloucester and Hereford, they were also employed on the Banbury & Cheltenham Direct line between Cheltenham and Kingham, where their duties included working the TC between Cheltenham and Paddington to and from Kingham. Worcester was the last home of the survivors of the class, Nos 3557 and 3559 being withdrawn in May 1934 and November 1931 respectively.

About half of the '3600' class 2-4-2Ts built in 1900-3 were employed on the Birmingham suburban services, though the only engine which appears to have been in the Worcester Division was No 3610 which was at Kidderminster in the mid-1920s. That shed also had 'Metro' class 2-4-0T No 976, this class having

61

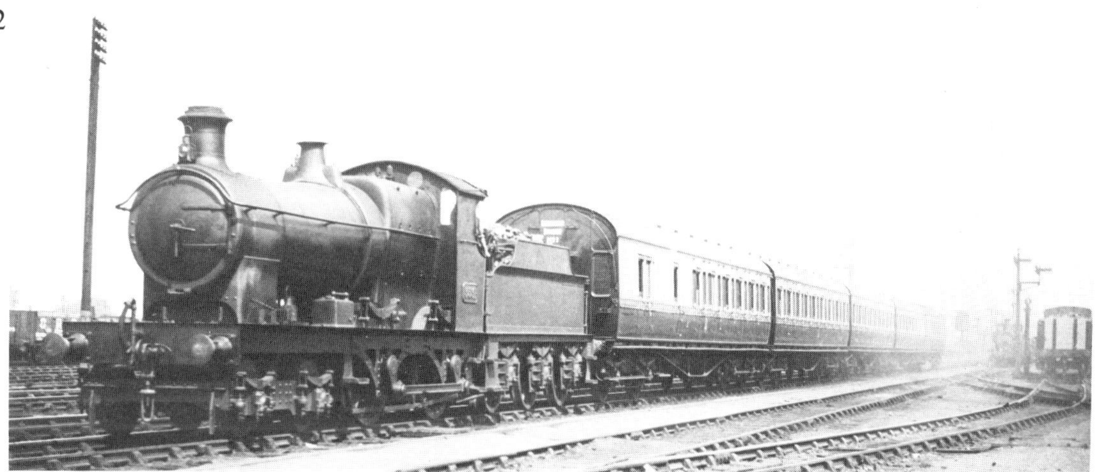

62

eventually managed to penetrate into the old Northern Division. There were also one or two of this class at Leamington, working through to Worcester.

Also at Kidderminster in the 1920s was one of the most unlikely and unusual engines ever to have been encountered in that area, the ex-Midland & South Western Junction Railway 4-4-4T No 18. One of a pair built by Sharp, Stewart in 1897, it had been renumbered by the GWR as No 27 and rebuilt with a new Standard No 10 superheated taper boiler; it was then sent to Kidderminster, from where it was withdrawn in 1929.

Another unusual class, both in origins and in appearance, of which one or two members were shedded at Worcester, was the '3901' class of inside cylinder 2-6-2Ts which had been 'converted' at Swindon from 'Dean Goods' 0-6-0s. Intended for service around Birmingham, and especially for the new North Warwickshire line, they became very familiar engines on the northern lines of the West Midland Section. However, the vast bulk of the local services,

some of which had now become auto-worked (though the GWR was still calling them rail motors), continued in the charge of the little '517' class 0-4-2Ts.

A few of the '3100' class 2-6-2Ts, from Wolverhampton, Stourbridge and the new Tyseley shed at Birmingham, also worked in the Worcester and Kidderminster areas. However, it was to be the small 2-6-2Ts of the '4575' class which were to effect a considerable change in the late 1920s, when many of them were sent as new engines to various sheds in the Worcester Division. They replaced worn-out tender and tank engines dating from the last century, and were to be found at Worcester, Hereford and Kidderminster. As more large 2-6-2Ts of the '5101' class were built, some began to appear in the Worcester area — Nos 4100 and 4114, built in 1935/6, being the first to be shedded at Worcester. The higher pressure engines of the '6100' class also turned up at Worcester from time to time on stopping trains from Oxford; and when the '8100' class (rebuilt from old '5100' class engines) appeared in 1938, No 8101 was sent to

Kidderminster, No 8103 to Stourbridge and No 8106 to Worcester.

The number of 'Bulldog' 4-4-0s had been greatly reduced in the 1930s; however, there were still three each at Worcester and Hereford in 1938, when Worcester also had No 3209, one of the 'new' hybrid 'Dukedog' engines. The little '517' class engines had by now disappeared from the area, having been replaced by their modern counterparts, the '4800' class; Worcester and Hereford having nine of these between them. Worcester had also acquired two of the last of the older Wolverhampton-built 0-4-2Ts of the '3571' class, Nos 3573 and 3574; while the former soon departed for other pastures (Swindon), No 3574 remained at Worcester for the rest of its days, sharing station pilot duties with the non-auto engines of the '58xx' series and also working on the Bromyard and Leominster service until withdrawn in 1949. Diesel railcars appeared in the area in the mid-1930s, working on both branch and main lines, and in 1947 there were seven shedded at Worcester. The intensive rostering of these vehicles involved some very complicated workings and duties.

Few of the ex-WMR goods engines had a very long life on the GWR and there was an early influx of newer engines. Some of these were Beyer, Peacock 0-6-0s of the '322' class, several of which were at Worcester in their early days, and Armstrong's

'Standard Goods' were also among the early arrivals. However, it was not until the early 1880s that the major replacement took place, when the withdrawal of many ex-WMR engines brought the advent of the 'Dean Goods' 0-6-0s in strength — Nos 2321-6, 2328-36, 2341-7, 2349 and 2350 all went as new engines to the Worcester District, where they promptly had their brass dome covers painted over: despite the domination by Wolverhampton, some West Midland traditions survived — and this was one of them! The double-framed engines of the '2361' class, built in 1885-6, also frequented the Worcester area in their early days.

Local goods and shunting duties were undertaken by 0-6-0STs built at Wolverhampton, the earlier ones having double frames. The only appearance of the similar Swindon-built engines was that of some of the '1076' class which worked on coal trains between Pontypool Road and Wolverhampton. During the 1890s, Hereford was the home of 0-6-0ST No 323, one of six engines rebuilt from the Beyer, Peacock 0-6-0s; most of these spent their later years at Stourbridge.

Three 'odd' little engines to be seen at Worcester during the early years of this century were ex-Whitland & Cardigan 0-6-0ST No 1385 *John Owen* (withdrawn and sold in 1912); 0-6-0T No 1357 *Maid Marian*, ex-Severn & Wye Valley Railway (withdrawn

**63**
'Dean Goods' No 2381 is on an up goods near
Stourbridge Junction.
*LGRP, courtesy David & Charles*

**64**
One of the first duties of the GWR's diesel railcars was
a through service from Oxford to Hereford. Diesel
railcar No 2 is seen on this working near Ledbury.
*LGRP, courtesy David & Charles*

in 1910); and No 1356 *Will Scarlet* was also
ex-Severn & Wye, and spent some time at Hereford
before moving to West Wales.

By the early 1930s many of the older 0-6-0s had
been withdrawn and the GWR universal 'maid of all
work', the '4300' class 2-6-0s, were present in small
numbers. However, there were still over 30 of the
'Dean Goods' in the Worcester Division in 1932, some
of which had been there since they were built; while
there were still no less than 16 at Worcester in 1938.
The double-framed engines of the '2361' class were
also fairly common, Nos 2363 (withdrawn October
1932), 2365 (withdrawn October 1928) and 2375
(withdrawn May 1938) being there in their later years.
The last 'Standard Goods' in the area was No 509
which was withdrawn from Hereford in 1930;
however, this was another class for which Stourbridge
acquired a fondness and a number of the last survivors
lasted there until 1934. Of the even older '131' class,
dating from 1862-5 (though 'renewed' in 1886-7),
No 139 was withdrawn from Hereford in 1919 and,
typically, Stourbridge was the last home of No 126
until withdrawn in 1921. The Beyer, Peacock 0-6-0s
were still around; indeed, in about 1920 No 329 had a
regular passenger turn from Hereford to Worcester!

With the advent of the new standard '5700' class
0-6-0PTs, many of the older tank engines disappeared.
The new engines were used on a wide range of duties,
from local passenger work to banking (at Ledbury and
Stourbridge) and shunting. Hereford also had one of
the smaller modern engines, No 7416, and there was
one of the similar auto-fitted engines, No 6430, at
Kidderminster. Other engines of the '6400' class were
to be found at Stourbridge, and these worked over the
main line to Wolverhampton as well as on local services such as Dudley to Old Hill.

However, many of the older engines soldiered on,
not least those of the small Wolverhampton '850' and
'2021' classes, of which a number were at both
Worcester and Hereford. One of the last two saddle
tanks, No 2007, spent its declining years at Worcester
where it was a familiar sight working on the Vinegar
Branch and the neighbouring coal yard line at Shrub
Hill.

The lines to both Wolverhampton and Birmingham
from Stourbridge had some severe gradients which
necessitated the banking of heavy freight trains, which
had been carried out for many years by various
0-6-0Ts, both 'saddles' and 'panniers'. During the
1930s, larger engines in the shape of 0-6-2Ts of the
'5600' class were sent to Stourbridge for this work and
for local freight duties.

With the withdrawal of the older 0-6-0s, four of the
modern '2251' class were sent to Worcester, while a
fifth engine was at Kidderminster — still without a
turntable despite having had a new shed in 1932! As
might have been expected, Stourbridge acquired a
number of the surviving 'Aberdare' class 2-6-0s; four
in 1938 — when Worcester and Hereford had one
each — and two in 1947, when there were also two at
Hereford. By 1938 Worcester had received its first
'2800' class 2-8-0, as well as a couple of 'ROD' class
engines, while the new 'Granges' were proving to be a
most useful mixed traffic engine — Nos 6807 *Birch-
wood Grange* and 6851 *Hurst Grange* being at
Worcester. The coal trains from Pontypool Road to
Wolverhampton and Birmingham still brought
numerous 2-8-0s, 2-8-0Ts and 2-8-2Ts on to the
Worcester and Hereford line and northwards to Stourbridge Junction.

The war years saw several engines owned by other
Companies being loaned to the GWR and working in
the Worcester area. LMS Class 2F (ex-Midland) and
LNER Class J25 (ex-North Eastern) 0-6-0s replaced
'Dean Goods' drafted to the War Department. USA
Army 2-8-0s, LMS '8F' 2-8-0s built at Swindon, and
'WD' 2-8-0s, all appeared in turn. Perhaps the most
unexpected visitors were a couple of ex-London,
Brighton & South Coast 4-4-2Ts of Class I3, which
had been kindly loaned by the Southern Railway for
local passenger duties.

# 7 'West to North' and 'North to West'

The western extremity of the WMR was the former NA&HR line southwards from Hereford to Pontypool Road, which for some years had only a local service between Hereford and Newport — the latter part of the journey being over the line of the Monmouthshire Railway. Though the opening of the Worcester to Hereford line in 1861 connected Hereford with the important industrial towns of Birmingham and Wolverhampton, little or no attempt was made at first to provide a through service to and from South Wales. Not only was the Monmouthshire's station at Newport quite separate from that of the GWR, the South Wales Railway through Newport and Cardiff was still a broad gauge line.

Three events brought about a great change in this situation and opened the way for the development of the former NA&HR line as part of an important cross-country main line. The first was the conversion in 1872 of the South Wales Railway to standard gauge — though there was still an awkward gap between Pontypool Road and the GWR at Newport. The second was the opening on the GWR's Pontypool, Caerleon & Newport Railway, on 17 September 1874, which filled in the 'gap'. This was followed by the introduction of daily through trains between Birmingham — but not Wolverhampton — and Cardiff, which also gave Worcester a through service to South Wales from Foregate Street.

North of Hereford, the jointly-owned S&HR line continued to provide an essential route for the export of coal from the Monmouthshire collieries: it also provided by far the most direct route for all traffic between South Wales and places north of Shrewsbury, but little attempt was made to develop the potential passenger traffic by through services. It was not until after 1886 that the full potential was realised; for on 1 September 1886, the Severn Tunnel was opened. In 1888 the GWR and LNWR entered into a new joint venture which made use of their joint ownership of the

S&HR and of the existence of the new route through the Severn Tunnel: this was the introduciton of a new express service between the North of England and Bristol.

Hitherto, the only means of travelling from Liverpool and Manchester to Bristol had remained firmly in the hands of the MR between Birmingham and Bristol. That Company sustained a severe shock when the new express service was inaugurated on 1 July 1888, beginning with three fast trains each way between Bristol and Crewe, which also connected South Wales as well as the West of England with the LNWR's main line. Through carriages to and from Liverpool, Manchester and Glasgow (Central) were introduced. There were also GWR TC serving Chester and Birkenhead. A year later, a fourth train was added to this service, which was the first cross-country service on the GWR.

It was not long before one train in each direction had yet another TC, this being to and from Leeds via Huddersfield, and within a few years others ran via Normanton to and from York, Darlington and Newcastle — this being a service to and from Cardiff.

One further event took place in May 1892, when the last citadel of the broad gauge west of Exeter finally surrendered and was converted to standard gauge. Through services to and from Torquay, Plymouth and Penzance were soon added to those to and from Bristol. There was also a daily through service between Plymouth and Glasgow, as well as Liverpool and Manchester, and at one time a TC between Bristol and Edinburgh (Princess Street). Not all these services survived to become established features in the Time Tables; some soon disappeared; others became confined to the summer months. In January 1902, the Time Tables showed only a daily through service between Glasgow and Plymouth, on the same train that conveyed TC from Liverpool and Manchester to Penzance — while there was no trace of any through

service in the northbound direction from either Penzance or Plymouth! Nor was there any reference to through services between the North of England and Torquay.

These trains were closely associated with the established through service between Birmingham and Cardiff, with which they were often combined south of Hereford. The Bristol and South Wales through services to and from the North were also combined north of Pontypool Road in a number of instances. However, the overnight services tended to be run separately to and from Shrewsbury. Thus both Pontypool Road and Hereford were the scene of considerable activity when trains were either combined or divided. As there was no consistency in this, some Bristol trains being combined with or divided from the Cardiff carriages at Pontypool Road, while others ran independently to or from Hereford (where the Birmingham and Cardiff TC were either attached or detached) it must have been rather confusing at times!

The West to North route was far from easy from the point of view of locomotive working. From Maindee Junction, Newport, to Pontypool Road there are nine miles of 1 in 126 to 1 in 96, followed by a six mile descent of 1 in 104 to 1 in 80. After Penpergwn there is a climb of 1 in 82 to Abergavenny, followed by 1 in 82 to 1 in 95 to the summit of Llanvihangel: a total rise of nine miles. Then follows a six mile fall of 1 in 100 to near Pontrilas, while the last five miles into Hereford are on a falling gradient of 1 in 105. From Hereford to Ludlow the line rises generally, though there are one or two slight falls; but after Ludlow there is another climb of 14 miles, of which $6\frac{1}{2}$ miles are at 1 in 100 to 1 in 112. Just south of Church Streeton this becomes a steep descent which continues for the $13\frac{1}{2}$ miles to Shrewsbury, much of this being at 1 in 90 to 1 in 100. Thus trains in both directions were faced with considerable climbs over several miles.

Double heading of trains was quite common,

**65**
2-4-0 No 442 of the '439' class piloting a 'County' class 4-4-0 on a train leaving Shrewsbury for the South. *Bucknall Collection/IAL*

especially in earlier days, while some of the heavier trains received banking assistance at the rear end up to Llanvihangel from either Pontypool Road or Abergavenny. From sturdy 0-6-0STs, the size of the 'bankers' increased until the '7200' class 2-8-2Ts could be seen — and heard — on such duties.

For many years the Birmingham and Cardiff through trains were worked by a handful of small 2-4-0s shedded at Hereford or at the original Birmingham shed at Bordesley. Those at Hereford, of the '111' class, have already been described; they also worked northwards to Shrewsbury and Chester on local trains. From Bordesley the engines used were of a quite different type, being inside-framed engines of the little-known '56' or '717' class built at Swindon in 1871-2. Nos 718, 721, 722, 723, 725 and 726 were at Bordesley for many years, where they were the only passenger tender engines (the other five engines of this class were at Weymouth for about 20 years). Prior to the opening of the Severn Tunnel, Cardiff had few, if any, main line passenger engines, and the few turns worked to Hereford or Worcester by that shed appear to have been in charge of 'Metro' class 2-4-0Ts.

However, the introduction of the first through trains between Bristol and Shrewsbury brought other engines to the line. The working of the new trains was shared between Bristol and Shrewsbury sheds, with engines and crews working through on each train: a practice which was to continue for nearly 50 years. Both sheds used 2-4-0s for these duties, but once again they were of very different types. Bristol used some of the rebuilt

66

**66**
No 3819 *County of Cardigan* leaving Shrewsbury on a local train for Hereford.  *H. M. Pearson*

**67**
No 2930 *Saint Vincent* heads a through train for South Wales and the West of England, south of Shrewsbury c1923.  *Real Photos*

**68**
0-6-0ST No 1994 and Beyer, Peacock 0-6-0 No 355 entering Shrewsbury on a goods train c1928.
*W. Potter*

67

68

engines of the '481' class, these being renewals in 1888-90 of engines built at Swindon in 1869; while those from Shrewsbury were Nos 149-52, which had outside sandwich-frames and had been built by George England & Co in 1862, as the very first standard gauge GWR 2-4-0s — though as 'renewed' at Wolverhampton between 1878 and 1883 very little of the original engines can have remained.

These small engines managed to cope with these duties for the first few years, but in 1893 larger engines were introduced: these were of the new '3232' class, being the last 2-4-0s built by the GWR. Some of these new engines were shedded at Bristol, a few others working south from Shrewsbury. However, they were not destined to enjoy a very long reign on these services, as within five years they had been replaced by much larger and more powerful engines. These were 4-4-0s of the 'Badminton' class, newly built at Swindon, and Nos 3300-11 were shedded at either Bristol or Shrewsbury for these duties — an indication of the importance which the GWR attached to these services. Later, some of the 'Atbara' class were also used.

The 'Badmintons' were responsible for some of the fastest and most exciting running ever known over the line. At the end of the last century, the GWR and LNWR in partnership ran what were known as 'Woolbuyers Special' trains from Bradford to Bristol. These were to enable the wool merchants from the North at attend the autumn wool sales held in Bristol — and the trains were in competition with the MR's direct route between Bradford and Bristol! Leaving Shrewsbury at 2.50pm the train was due in Bristol at 5.17pm, while the northbound train leaving Bristol at 4.30pm was due at Shrewsbury at 6.55pm. In each direction the train consisted of five carriages, including two dining cars. Between Shrewsbury and Hereford speeds of nearly 80mph were recorded on these trains when hauled by No 3301 *Monarch*.

The overnight service in both directions was always of great importance, and in 1902 it provided the only advertised through service from Glasgow to Plymouth and from the North of England to Penzance. There was no service in either direction on Sunday nights. The southbound service was unusual for that time in running as separate trains for the West of England and South Wales from Shrewsbury; only a Birkenhead to Cardiff train, with no TC for Bristol, was similarly distinguished. The latter left Shrewsbury at 2.20pm and stopped at the principal stations to Hereford — another unusual feature — and it was the only daytime service not to convey TC from Birmingham to Cardiff forward from Hereford.

The overnight service was: Shrewsbury (dep 2.15am); Hereford (3.23am/3.33am); Bristol (arr 5.15am); TC Glasgow to Plymouth (arr 10.50am); TC

Liverpool and Manchester to Penzance (arr 2.47pm); Shrewsbury (dep 2.35am); Hereford (3.43/3.53am); Pontypool Road ('to set down passengers only'); Cardiff (arr 5.38am); TC Liverpool and Newcastle to Cardiff. As none of the trains between the North of England and South Wales or the West of England were advertised as having corridor carriages, the 10min stop at Hereford was of considerable importance!

Four trains with TC for both Bristol and Cardiff left Shrewsbury during the day: in each instance TC from Birmingham to Cardiff were attached at Hereford. These trains had a variety of combinations of through carriages, with one or two of them living up to Ahron's classic description of the whole service as 'a profusion of through coaches from everywhere to everywhere else'.

Northbound, the first departure of the day was from Bristol at 1.20am and from Cardiff at 1.30am, both trains running non-stop to Hereford according to the Time Tables: however, as both arrived at 3.00am, there must have been a service stop to combine the trains at Pontypool Road. The Bristol train probably conveyed TC from Penzance to Liverpool and Manchester, while the TC from Plymouth to Glasgow went north from Bristol at 7.40pm. The Time Tables gave no details of northbound TC from Bristol, except to state that they were 'run on all the principal services'. Two of the trains from Bristol actually commenced from Weston-Super-Mare at 12.05pm and 4.10pm; the former had TC to Birkenhead, Manchester, Liverpool and Leeds, while the latter had TC to Birkenhead, Liverpool and Manchester. The first of these trains provided a classic example of 'good' planning, as it arrived at Hereford 5min after the TC from Cardiff to Birmingham had departed!

There was a considerable increase in traffic during World War 1, partly due to travel between the industrial areas of Lancashire and South Wales. Some of the Birmingham and Cardiff trains were withdrawn in 1917 owing to wartime pressures. A wartime practice was the combining of the West of England and South Wales portions on some northbound trains at Maindee North Junction, just outside Newport; the southbound trains appear to have been divided as formerly, at either Hereford or Pontypool Road.

By 1932, there were six trains daily in each direction, with a considerable number of extra trains on Fridays and Saturdays in the summer. The southbound overnight train to Cardiff now left Shrewsbury at 2.20am, ahead of the West of England train which left at 2.35am. However, on Monday mornings the two were combined as far as Pontypool Road. The Bristol train stopped for 15min at Hereford, after which it ran non-stop to arrive at Temple Meads at 5.30am. The Time Tables stated 'Passengers

69

70

can obtain breakfast at Bristol on giving notice to the Guard at Hereford'. This train conveyed 'through carriages from the North of England to Plymouth and Penzance', also a TC from Glasgow (dep 5.30pm) to Plymouth (arr 10.05am). Departure from Bristol was at 6.15am.

The final train of the day, the 9.20pm from Shrewsbury, spent 15min at Hereford and then ran non-stop to Newport, reached at 11.46pm. The Cardiff carriages reached their destination at 12.14am, while those for Bristol formed the 11.54pm from Newport to Temple Meads. There was, however, some uncertainty as to when exactly it was due at the latter station, the

time depending on which page in the Time Tables was consulted. According to the 'North of England, South Wales and West of England' pages, it was at 12.30am, while those for the South Wales to Bristol and London services stated that it was at 12.34am!

There was now a daytime train on Sundays in addition to the overnight service. This was a Restaurant Car train from Manchester to Plymouth, which left Shrewsbury at 12.50pm. Bristol was reached via Newport, where the train was combined with the 1.05pm from Swansea to Bristol, arriving at Temple Meads at 4.05pm, and the Manchester carriages reached Plymouth at 8.17pm.

**69**

No 5030 *Shirburn Castle* (of Cardiff shed) heads the 8.45am Plymouth to Liverpool and Manchester through train, with through carriages from Cardiff, passing Onibury — a typical rural station on the Shrewsbury & Hereford Joint line, 1951.
*C. R. L. Coles*

**70**

A resplendent 'Castle' No 5046 *Earl Cawdor*, another Cardiff engine, is in charge of the 3.00pm Liverpool to Cardiff and Manchester to Plymouth through train, seen at Marshbrook in 1951.   *C. R. L. Coles*

**71**

Also at Marshbrook, but in 1933, No 5905 *Knowsley Hall* heads a 'North to West' express.
*Dr Ian C. Allen*

The northbound service was notable in having more trains leaving the West of England than ever arrived there! The 12.23pm from Bristol and the 12.35pm from Cardiff were combined at Pontypool Road, and only 4min were allowed at Hereford — during which a Cardiff to Birmingham portion had to be detached! This must have called for some very smart station work. Other trains having no such work involved were allowed anything from 7 to 10min at Hereford! The inclusion of TC from Cardiff to Birmingham was now the exception rather than the rule. The 11.50pm from Bristol, with TC for Manchester and Liverpool from Penzance (dep 5.05pm) was routed via Newport (arr

12.28am) and was there combined with the 12.05am from Cardiff before leaving at 12.38am to run non-stop to Hereford.

On Sundays, both the northbound trains from Bristol were combined at Newport with TC from Cardiff. The 10.20am Plymouth to Manchester (RC from Newton Abbot) had TC from Cardiff to Liverpool attached, while the Paignton to Manchester train (again with RC) also had TC from Cardiff to Liverpool.

There were now only three trains in each direction between Birmingham and Cardiff, though there was now also one each via Stratford-on-Avon and Cheltenham. There was still no through service on Sundays.

The weight of the through trains having increased considerably during the early years of this century, there was a desire to introduce much larger engines. However, the GWR suffered from the partnership with the LNWR as far as the line north of Hereford was concerned, and that company resolutely refused to countenance the use of engines of the 'Saint' class on these services. This resulted in the continued use of 4-4-0s, but as these were now of the outside cylinder 'County' class — Churchward's 'Rough Riders' — the permanent way probably suffered more than it would have done had the 'Saints' been allowed! Regular use of the 'Counties' did not commence until c1909 and it lasted until the mid-1920s. From about 1916 'Saints' took over many of these duties and were joined in the 1920s by the 'Stars' and some of the first 'Halls'. Pontypool Road was one of the first sheds of lesser importance to have 'Saints' allocated — the first arriving as early as 1923, when there was also one at Shrewsbury. By 1932, the advent of 'Saints' at Newport and Hereford made it possible for the duties

**72**
'Star' class No 4046 *Princess Mary* passing Craven Arms on a 'North to West' express in 1933. *Dr Ian C. Allen*

**73**
No 6352 heads an up Shrewsbury stopper at Ashford Bowdler in 1951. *C. R. L. Coles*

**74**
Freight traffic was always of great importance on the 'West to North' line. No 2829 is on an up train at Ashford Bowdler in 1951. *C. R. L. Coles*

to be more widely shared; though Bristol and Hereford continued to share the major responsibility, Cardiff engines and crews were also employed. Cardiff had 14 'Saints' in 1923, and there were still 10 shedded there in 1932 — when Newport had three, Pontypool Road two, and Hereford one.

Shrewsbury received its first 'Stars' in about 1931, and by the following year were no less than 11 shedded there. As Bristol had 13, the 'Saints' were no longer the premier engines on the line. 'Castles' were also introduced, together with 'double home' workings between Newton Abbot and Shrewsbury, involving engines and crews from both sheds, during the 1930s.

The first two 'Castles' allocated to Shrewsbury had arrived by 1935, and by 1947 there were eight there; however, 'Stars' continued to be the mainstay of that shed's express allocation, there still being 10 there in 1938.

Cardiff's 'Saints', of which there were still seven in 1938, continued to work the majority of the turns to Hereford, though 'Castles' were also employed. Hereford became a great centre for 'Saints', its prewar allocation of two engines having been increased to eight in the final days of the GWR. They performed legendary feats during the war years, taking 16 or 17 carriages unaided over the Hereford to Shrewsbury section on

equal terms with the 'Castles', and became known locally as 'Hereford Castles'.

The war years again brought a great increase in the number of passengers using these services; in this case it was due largely to the movement of naval personnel and merchant seamen between Plymouth or South Wales and Merseyside. Unlike many other cross-country services, which were either drastically reduced or withdrawn entirely, the 'West to North' and 'North to West' were maintained at full strength, though TC to and from Birkenhead disappeared.

The final Time Tables of the GWR, for the winter of 1947, still retained the overnight services to South Wales and the West of England. The Cardiff train, with TC from Manchester and Liverpool, still left Shrewsbury at 2.20am; but the West of England train now left at 3.00am, this being the 12.30am Manchester to Penzance service. Bristol was reached at 6.00am and there was a 45min stop, presumably for breakfast — though there was no mention in the Time Tables of the need to inform the Guard at Hereford — Penzance being reached at 1.40pm. Two other trains had TC only for Bristol and the West of England: the 9.15am Liverpool to Kingswear (arr 7.08pm) and Penzance (arr 10.30pm) leaving Shrewsbury at 11.45am, and the 12.15pm Manchester to Plymouth which left Shrewsbury at 2.25pm and arrived at Plymouth at 10.05pm. All daytime TC for Cardiff were combined with those for the West of England.

However, from 'West to North', most trains ran separately throughout: indeed, there were only two combined services. The first of these was the early morning train, leaving Bristol at 8.15am and Cardiff at 8.20am with TC for Manchester, which combined at Pontypool Road. The second combined the 1.00pm Plymouth to Liverpool (Bristol dep 4.30pm) and the 4.55pm Cardiff to Manchester services, only 4min being allowed for this purpose at Pontypool Road.

On Sundays there were no TC from Manchester to Cardiff on the overnight service, while the Bristol train left at 2.45am and had TC for Plymouth instead of Penzance. A through train from Manchester to Cardiff left Shrewsbury at 1.12pm and was followed at 1.35pm by a through train to Plymouth with TC from Manchester and Liverpool — this was allowed 45min at Bristol, probably to enable passengers to get a meal, as there was no RC, and Plymouth was reached at 9.40pm.

There was no less than four northbound trains on Sundays, including the overnight trains from Penzance to Manchester and from Cardiff to Liverpool. The 12.40pm Cardiff to Manchester arrived at Shrewsbury at 3.42pm, being closely followed by the 7.05am Plymouth to Liverpool (Bristol dep 12.35pm) which was due at 4.00pm. There was a similar succession of evening trains, with the 6.00pm Cardiff to Manchester arriving at Shrewsbury at 8.55pm and the 5.40pm Bristol to Liverpool arriving at 9.35pm. The latter provided a service for Leominster, Woofferton, Ludlow, Craven Arms and Church Stretton — the only through train in either direction to do so.

During the winter months, from November to March (with a short break over Christmas and the New Year), the Bristol trains in both directions were diverted on Sundays via Gloucester and Hereford, as the Severn Tunnel was closed for engineering work. The 4.45pm Penzance to Manchester did not run on Sundays, the service commencing from Bristol.

The Birmingham and Cardiff through service has not been increased and some trains still ran at almost the same times as in 1902; though there was now a fourth train from Birmingham to Cardiff on Saturdays. One feature which persisted over the years was the absence of any afternoon train from Cardiff to Birmingham, though one left Birmingham for Cardiff at 5.00pm. However, there were now two trains in

75

76

78

Further south on the same line, in evening sunlight
'ROD' class No 3042 at the head of a down freight
descends Llanvihangel Bank in 1953.  *R. C. Riley*


Northbound trains faced a stiff climb for several miles
after leaving Abergavenny. No 6872 *Crawley Grange*
climbs the bank at Llanvihangel, on a northbound
express.  *P. M. Alexander/Colourviews Ltd*

each direction via Stratford-on-Avon and Cheltenham,
and there was now a service on Sundays! This consisted of an early morning train from Cardiff (dep
7.20am), which called at most stations to Pontypool
Road, Abergavenny, Pontrilas, and the usual stations
between Hereford and Birmingham (arr 11.55am);
while from Birmingham there was an afternoon train
(dep 4.50pm) which made only the normal stops on
this service, reaching Cardiff at 9.12pm.

The NA&HR was very much more concerned with
coal than with passengers, while cross-country express
trains were far more the minds of the original promoters of the S&HR. In 1902, there were seven stopping trains from Hereford to Shrewsbury, two of
which had TC from Cheltenham; while there were
eight in the reverse direction, of which the 6.50am
from Shrewsbury had TC for Gloucester. One or two
local trains ran between Hereford and Craven Arms,
and between Shrewsbury and Ludlow; while the
LNWR had a few between Shrewsbury and Craven
Arms for its Central Wales line. There was also a
handful of trains between Leominster and Ludlow in
connection with the service to and from Tenbury
Wells. On Sundays there was but one train in each
direction, that from Hereford leaving at 10.30am and
that from Shrewsbury at 5.00pm. The former appears
to have been a through train from Newport.

There were four trains daily between Hereford and
Newport, but only three in the reverse direction. The
service on Sundays consisted of the 8.00am from
Newport (probably through to Shrewsbury), and the
7.50pm from Hereford, both of which used the old
Monmouthshire line south of Pontypool Road.

There was little change in the local service during
the remainder of the GWR's existence. By 1932, the
local trains between Leominster and Ludlow were
auto-worked, and on Sundays there were now two
trains in each direction between Cardiff and
Shrewsbury which served such stations as were open.
In 1947, the pattern was almost identical with that in
1932.

The engines employed over the years between
Shrewsbury and Hereford on the local services were of
great variety — both in origins and appearance. The
line was truly a 'joint' one, as both the GWR and the
LNWR provided engines and rolling stock. There was
often the spectacle of GWR engines heading trains of
LNWR carriages, and of engines whose origins could
be none other than Crewe on trains of carriages which
had obviously been built at Swindon. Needless to say,
neither Company provided their latest products, either
in engines or rolling stock! In the 19th century there
was a succession of GWR 2-4-0s, the earlier ones
being of WMR origin. LNWR 2-4-0s of
Ramsbottom's designs were followed in the early years
of this century by most classes of Webb's Compounds
in quick succession.

Following the various 2-4-0s, the GWR made use of
the 4-4-0s which had been demoted from express
working, including several of the immortal 'Cities' —
*City of Truro* and *Killarney* were at Shrewsbury and
employed on such local working prior to their withdrawal. They were followed by the '4300' class 2-6-0s,
'Saints', 'Stars' and 'Halls'. The general massacre of
the Webb Compounds saw 'Precedent' 2-4-0s, the
rebuilt 'Renown' class 4-4-0s and 'Experiment' class
4-6-0s, used by the LNWR; while in LMS days, it was
the turn of the 'Prince of Wales' 4-6-0s until the advent
of the all-conquering Stanier 'Black Fives'.

Coal traffic was the life blood of the NA&HR and
continued to be so, despite the through services.
Though the line from Hereford to Shrewsbury was the
natural outlet, a considerable amount of this traffic
also flowed over the line to Worcester and on to the
great industrial centres of Wolverhampton and
Birmingham. Until May 1871, GWR coal trains from
Aberdare to London and Basingstoke also ran via
Hereford, Worcester and Oxford, there being four or
five trains daily. In August 1871, standard gauge
goods services between Bristol and Birmingham and
Birkenhead were introduced; these used the MR line to
Gloucester, then ran over the Gloucester to Hereford
line.

The most important traffic was that to and from
Birkenhead, which was not only an important port for
the export of coal; it was also responsible for a considerable traffic in imported iron ore. Much of the
latter was destined for the iron works and foundries of
Monmouthshire and South Wales, and this traffic to a
certain extent balanced the northbound traffic in coal.
However, the widespread use of 'private owners'
wagons, from a variety of collieries, meant that long
trains of empty coal wagons had to be worked south
from Shrewsbury.

Originally this traffic had been worked by outside-
framed or double-framed 0-6-0s — NA&HR engines
working through to Chester by arrangement. Pontypool Road shed used either the '79' class or the '322'
class: the former were small-wheeled versions of

Gooch's original standard gauge goods engines, while the latter were built at Gorton by Beyer, Peacock Ltd. With curved frames and characteristic Beyer, Peacock brass rims to the splashers, they were among the most handsome engines of their type to run on the GWR. Swindon-built 0-6-0STs of the '1076' class were employed between Pontypool Road and Wolverhampton, a distance of 98 miles!

Birkenhead shed used engines of '927' class, small-wheeled versions of Armstrong's 'Standard Goods' class; the great majority of this class were always shedded at Birkenhead and used on these duties. They were known as 'Coal Engines', which must have caused some confusion at times at both Shrewsbury and Birkenhead; at both places the GWR and LNWR sheds stood side by side — and the latter Company used Webb's 'Coal Engines' on similar duties to and from Monmouthshire!

Eventually, the old 'Beyers' and 'Coal Engines' handed over their trains to larger engines. In the 1920s, the double-framed 'Aberdare' class 2-6-0s were employed, being followed by the '2800' and 'ROD' classes of 2-8-0s. As well as working regularly to Wolverhampton, the '4200' class 2-8-0Ts also worked on occasions to Shrewsbury. These heavy northbound coal trains required banking up the long gradient from Abergavenny to Llanvihangel, and a couple of tank engines were shedded at Abergavenny for this work. The original pair of NA&HR saddle tanks (GWR Nos 235 and 236) were withdrawn in 1877, two other absorbed engines taking over these duties. These were Nos 413 and 414, double-framed 0-6-0STs built by Stephenson's in 1864, for the Vale of Neath Railway.

**77**
At the south end of the 'West to North' route, 'Saint' class No 2987 *Bride of Lammermoor* pilots a 'Grange' out of Newport station in the late 1930s. In postwar days No 2987 was one of many 'Saints' shedded at Hereford; in 1938 it was shedded at Cardiff.
*Rail Archive Stephenson*

Following their withdrawal in 1884-5, standard double-framed saddle tanks were employed. In 1926, Nos 958 and 1614 of the Swindon-built '1076' class and No 1039 of the Wolverhampton '1016' class were at Abergavenny. The shed was closed in 1932.

Banking duties having been taken over by eight-coupled engines, it was possible to witness the great combination of a '2800' class 2-8-0 on the front of a northbound coal train and a mighty '7200' class 2-8-2T pounding away at the rear. This was a sight and sound never to be forgotten, and as memorable as other features of the line — the 'Fairy Tale' castle at Stokesay; the Long Mynd covered in snow and bathed in winter sunlight, with Newton Abbot's 'Castle' No 7000 *Viscount Portal* descending the bank from Church Stretton into Shrewsbury at the head of a train of immaculate chocolate and cream carriages; and the boards of all those through trains, with Liverpool, Manchester and Glasgow, Plymouth, Kingswear and Penzance, Newport and Cardiff, as a moving catalogue of the 'West to North' and 'North to West' services.

# 8 Branches in Oxfordshire and Worcestershire ('Cotswold Country')

**Oxford to Witney and Fairford**

The origins of this well-known branch, which ultimately extended from Yarnton to the East Gloucestershire town of Fairford, famous for the medieval glass in its parish church, a distance of just under 22 miles, was to be found in one of the minor railways which the WMR undertook to work when completed. This was the Witney Railway, eight miles long, to the important blanket-making town, which was opened on 18 November 1861. The original powers granted to the OW&WR in 1846 had included a $4\frac{1}{2}$-mile branch to Witney, which had never been undertaken. It was a single track line, with intermediate stations at Eynsham and South Leigh. The initial service was of four trains daily, though this was later increased to five in each direction. Being a town of some importance for both passenger and goods traffic — the latter largely blankets and agricultural produce — Witney had a fairly large station, though this had only one platform, and a small engine shed.

The undramatic origins and opening of this line gave little hint of the trouble which was soon to arise at its western end. This was the struggle over the East Gloucestershire Railway (related in Chapter 3), whose grandiose scheme was eventually reduced to an extension of the Witney Railway as far as Fairford; however, plans for a further extension to Cheltenham were still being talked about in 1922!

The extension involved the closure to passengers of the original Witney station, which continued to be used for goods traffic until the end of the GWR's existence; the extension being from a new station which had two platforms, with a signalbox on the up platform. The new line was just over 14 miles long and was opened on 15 January 1873. There were intermediate stations at Brize Norton and Bampton (originally Bampton (Oxon) to distinguish it from Bampton in Devon). Alvescot and Lechlade were opened early in this century, while an additional station and signalbox were opened at Carterton in 1944, to serve the large airfield nearby.

With the closure of the original Witney station to passengers came also the closure of the engine shed there — though the building was not demolished until November 1905. A shed was now provided at the new terminus at Fairford, where the layout was rather unusual; the goods shed, crossing loop and engine shed were all to the west of the station — which had only one platform: it was almost as though the extension to Cheltenham had been commenced and then abandoned!

The branch was of considerable interest from the locomotive aspect, being the last haunt of several notable classes of engines. In the early years of this century, these included some of the last Single-wheelers on the GWR — their use being made possible by the existence of a turntable at Fairford. The last two members of the '55' or 'Queen' class, Nos 1124 and 1128, found employment on the branch until withdrawn in June 1912 and April 1914 respectively. No 1128 was fitted with ATC gear in 1906 in connection with the first experiments with this apparatus which were carried out on the branch. Another engine so equipped was the last surviving member of the '157' class, No 165, which lasted until December 1914 — having outlived the rest of the class by eight years and being the last GWR 2-2-2. 'River' class 2-4-0s were probably also used at the turn of the century, as all eight were at Oxford when newly reconstructed in the 1890s.

Although 0-6-0STs were sometimes used, it was the 2-4-0Ts of the 'Metro' class which for many years were associated with this line. A considerable number of these engines was to be found at Oxford in the 1920s, and among the last survivors Nos 3562, 3585, 3588 and 3589 all worked on the Fairford branch — No 3588 being the last of the class to be withdrawn, in December 1949. In the early years, the '517' class

WITNEY
7436

**78**

For many years the 'Metro' 2-4-0Ts were associated with the Oxford-Fairford line. No 3585 stands in the bay at Oxford Station on the 4.22pm to Fairford, 1 June 1935. The third carriage appears to have been the victim of some over-zealous shunting! No 3585 was withdrawn from Oxford shed in January 1948. *W. Potter*

**79**

Successor to the 'Metro' tanks were the '7400' class 0-6-0PTs. No 7436, in charge of an Oxford to Fairford train, replenishes its tanks while standing at Witney, 14 May 1951. *R. C. Riley*

**80**

Journey's end. Fairford engine shed was the furthest point west on the branch which never managed to extend to Cheltenham. No 7436 creates a pall of smoke over the East Gloucestershire countryside. 14 May 1951. *R. C. Riley*

0-4-2Ts were used. The normal engines used on goods turns for many years were the 'Dean Goods' 0-6-0s, especially No 2579 which monopolised the workings for some considerable time. In about 1926, the little 2-4-0s acquired by the GWR from the M&SWJR were tried out on goods turns, and in later years the '2251' class were also to be found on this work — and on passenger duties. The '7400' class 0-6-0PTs shared the passenger workings with the 'Metro' engines, and were their eventual successors; Nos 7411 and 7412 were the engines allocated to Fairford on 31 December 1947. '4800' class 0-4-2Ts were also used at times just prior to World War 2.

In 1902, the train service consisted of five trains in each direction, with an additional train from Oxford to Witney and back on Thursday Only (the return working from Witney, at 5.30pm, being 'Mixed'). The first train was from Fairford at 7.15am, the first from Oxford not being until 9.10am. The last departure from Fairford was at 6,35pm, returning from Oxford at 9.40pm and reaching Fairford at 10.45pm. On Sundays there was one train each way, leaving Oxford at 4.15pm and Fairford at 6.20pm. However, by 1914 there was a morning and afternoon train in both directions.

By 1932, there were two additional trains from Oxford to Bampton and back, also two Saturday Only return workings between Oxford and Witney. As well as the early morning train from Fairford (dep 7.05am) there was now also a 7.57am from Oxford (the trains crossing at Yarnton); this returned from Bampton at

8.47am and crossed with the 9.18am Oxford to Fairford (at Witney). It was thus necessary for Fairford to have two engines shedded there overnight. The last trains from Oxford and Fairford were at similar time to those in 1902; however, on Saturdays there was an 11.00pm from Oxford to Witney, returning from there at 11.35pm. There was once again only one train in each direction on Sundays, at almost the same times as in 1902.

In 1947, the service had improved a little, as there were now six trains in each direction, with a seventh from Oxford to Carterton and back — this being by auto-train, as was the first departure from Oxford at 8.00am. From Fairford there was still an early morning train (now leaving at 6.35am) and a second train at 9.15am; the first crossed with the 8.00am auto-train between Oxford and Yarnton, while the second crossed with the 9.28am from Oxford (return working of the 6.35am from Fairford) at Witney. The last train from Fairford was now at 6.10pm and that from Oxford was a little later than in former years — probably for the benefit of Forces personnel — leaving at 10.10pm to arrive at Fairford at 11.35pm. On Sundays, there were now two trains in each direction, these being worked from Fairford and leaving there at 9.06am and 6.36pm, the return workings from Oxford being at 11.25am and 10.35pm. The latter train provided the unusual feature of a later service on Sundays than on weekdays, and did not arrive at Fairford until midnight.

**Branches from Chipping Norton Junction (Kingham)**

Chipping Norton Junction station owed its existence to the fact that the main line passed within a few miles of an important market and milling town. The branch line to Chipping Norton, $4\frac{1}{2}$ miles long, was opened on 10 August 1855, being the first branch line opened by the OW&WR who provided an initial service of three trains in each direction. The station at Chipping Norton Junction was of modest dimensions, and provided a simple bay line, with a run-round loop, behind the up platform, for the use of the branch trains.

On 1 March 1862, another branch line was opened from the junction, this time southwards to Bourton-on-the-Water, a distance of $6\frac{1}{2}$ miles. There was one intermediate station at Stow-on-the-Wold, thus providing the improbable sequence of Chipping Norton Junction, Stow-on-the-Wold and Bourton-on-the-Water! Originally provided with four trains each way, the service was later increased to five or six trains — the number of trains on the Chipping Norton branch having also been increased.

Despite the advent of the new branch there was no enlargement of the station at the junction, and from the layout trains to and from Bourton had to use the up main line and platform, there being no direct access to the down line. At Chipping Norton itself there was a fairly large goods yard and a small engine shed. The layout at the other branch terminus was simpler and there appears to have been no engine shed provided; though how the branch was worked without one is difficult to imagine, as there was no shed at Chipping Norton Junction until 1881.

Both these branches might have maintained an undisturbed existence for many years, but for the GWR's decision to construct what was known as the Banbury & Cheltenham Direct Line. This was to use both branches, with a new line southwards from Bourton to Cheltenham (proposed some years earlier in connection with the East Gloucestershire Railway) and another northwards from Chipping Norton to King's Sutton on the main line from Oxford to Banbury. In the event, it was the southern section which was constructed first, the $16\frac{1}{2}$ miles from Lansdown Junction at Cheltenham being opened on 1 June 1881. It was a single line with four intermediate stations, each having two platforms and a passing loop. There was a stretch of line rising at 1 in 60 to Notgrove in either direction. Bourton-on-the-Water was provided with a new up platform, but the original single platforms was retained at Stow-on-the-Wold.

The northern section, from King's Sutton to Chipping Norton, was not opened until almost six years later, on 6 April 1887. The $15\frac{1}{2}$ miles of single line had the same number of intermediate stations as the southern section. As at Witney, the extension involved the closure of the original passenger station at Chipping Norton, a new one being built to the north of the original premises which remained in use as the goods station.

Chipping Norton Junction was now quite inadequate for the increased volume of traffic, and was reconstructed to provide direct access from both the former branches to and from the main lines. The former bay was extended, the line joining the up main line beyond the platform, and an additional platform provided on the north side of the branch run-round loop. Access from the Cheltenham line to the new double track behind the up platform was made possible by the provision of cross-overs etc. At the same time as the Cheltenham line had been opened, a small engine shed had been built in the space between the main lines and the line to Chipping Norton, access to the shed being by means of a turntable situated on a short siding.

Little more was done until the early years of this century, despite the fact that the Banbury & Cheltenham Direct was a misnomer — as direct running was in no way possible! However, in 1906 the Direct Loop was opened, which by-passed the station and crossed the main line by means of an overbridge to the north west of the station. This was a double track line, as were both lines from the station, but became single track after the junctions at the West and East signalboxes. Chipping Norton Junction was unique on the GWR in having four signalboxes named after the four points of the compass! The engine shed was partially demolished in 1906; but engines continued to be turned and stabled there, a new shed being erected in 1913. By that time both the station and the engine shed had been renamed Kingham.

The original engines employed on the two short branches were the pair of delightful little 2-2-2Ts, Nos 52 and 53, known as 'Mr and Mrs Johnson'. When these were withdrawn in 1877-8, they were replaced by the usual '517' 0-4-2Ts which continued to work the services for some years, even after the opening of the extensions. Although the service to Bourton became part of that to and from Cheltenham, Chipping Norton continued to have a number of trains which ran to and from that station. These were still being worked by the '517' class in this century, No 575 being shedded at Chipping Norton in 1901 — when the engine at the junction shed was 0-6-0ST No 1861: most unusually for the West Midland Section, this was of Swindon origin, being of the '1854' class. The Banbury to Chipping Norton Junction service appears to have been worked by Banbury's No 849 — fated to be withdrawn in April 1904, the first of the '517' class to be scrapped.

Chipping Norton shed closed in 1922, after which the engine for the local service was provided by Kingham. By the late 1920s the service had been considerably reduced and partly replaced by a bus service (full details being shown in the Time Tables). The only engine at Kingham in 1938 was a 'Dean Goods' 0-6-0, and there was none there in 1947. The southern section was worked from Cheltenham, using either '517' class 0-4-2Ts or 'Metro' class 2-4-0Ts. However, by the 1920s the '3521' class 4-4-0s were being used, and later '4500' class 2-6-2Ts were employed. The Banbury at Kingham section had become entirely auto-worked in the 1920s. The only regular through train was that between Newcastle and Swansea (originally Barry), successively worked by 'Bulldogs', '4300' class 2-6-0s, and — from 1938 — the new 'Manor' class of lightweight 4-6-0s.

In 1902, there were 10 trains in each direction between the junction and Chipping Norton, two of these being mixed. The first train left Chipping Norton at 7.46am, while the last departure from Chipping Norton Junction was at 9.35pm. There were four trains each way between Banbury and Chipping Norton Junction, and five on the southern section to and from Cheltenham. Of the latter, the 11.40am from Cheltenham and the 3.40pm from the junction stopped only at Bourton, having TC to and from Paddington. By 1932, there were only two trains between Kingham

81

**81**

'Bulldog' No 3417 *Lord Mildmay of Flete* and No 7810 *Draycott Manor* — the latter engine only a few months old — leaving Banbury on the Newcastle to Swansea through train in 1939. *Ian Allan Library*

**82**

The South Wales to Newcastle through train, headed by a '4300' class 2-6-0, leaves the direct loop at Kingham, 6 September 1922. *H. G. W. Household*

**83**

Adderbury, the most northerly station on the Banbury & Cheltenham direct line, owed its importance to the adjacent iron stone quarry. No 5313, on a freight train for Banbury, passes through the station after its closure to passengers in 1951. *R. C. Riley*

82

83

and Chipping Norton, and rail motors — or auto-trains — provided four return workings from Banbury to Kingham. There were five trains in each direction between Kingham and Cheltenham, the 2.22pm from Kingham having TC from Paddington (dep 12.45pm) to Cheltenham.

However modest, there was now a service on Sundays, this being the 3.50pm rail motor from Banbury to Notgrove (the next station after Bourton), which returned from there at 5.25pm. On weekdays there was the Newcastle and Swansea through service which used the avoiding line.

The situation in 1947 was much the same as in 1932; though the bus services between Banbury and Kingham were no longer shown in the Time Tables, and the only Kingham and Chipping Norton trains were a return trip by a diesel railcar leaving Kingham at 2.20pm (an extension of the 1.25pm service from Oxford) and one by an ordinary train leaving Kingham at 4.00pm and returning from Chipping Norton at 4.35pm. The latter was provided by the engine and carriages of the 2.45pm from Cheltenham, which returned from Kingham at 5.15pm. Four trains, all of ordinary stock, ran in each direction between Cheltenham and Kingham, while the Banbury to Kingham service consisted of four return trips by an auto-train worked by a '4800' class 0-4-2T.

**The Shipston-on-Stour Branch**

This was the last of the branches to be opened between Oxford and Worcester, and was the first to be closed to passengers; though as a goods line it had claim to have had the longest life. The Stratford & Moreton Railway was an ancient horse-drawn tramway between Stratford-on-Avon and Moreton-in-the-Marsh, with a branch to Shipston-on-Stour, which was authorised in 1821. The gauge was 4ft, the fish-bellied rails being laid on stone blocks. It was the fortune of the Company to have the course of the OW&WR so laid out that it cut right through their terminus at Moreton, and a perpetual lease of the tramway by the Railway Company was agreed in 1844. As, at that time, the expenses for several years had averaged about £400 more than the receipts, it was indeed good fortune!

The OW&WR continued to work the line — and to incur an annual loss, which by 1865 was over £1,600. Goods traffic was conveyed by the traders themselves, who were also allowed to take passengers on their wagons on the payment of £1 per month for a licence.

**84**

A single auto-trailer normally sufficed for the traffic between Kingham and Banbury. A '4800' class 0-4-2T propels its carriage away from Chipping Norton station and into the tunnel, in 1936. *C. R. L. Coles*

**85**

4-4-0 No 3525 of the '3521' class heads the 3.12pm Kingham to Cheltenham near Charlton Kings, 5 July 1924. The rear three carriages had been slipped at Kingham from the 1.30pm Paddington-Hereford express. *H. G. W. Household*

**86**

'Metro' 2-4-0T No 628 is in charge of a Cheltenham-Kingham train near Charlton Kings, 5 April 1924. Built in 1871, No 628 was not withdrawn from service until March 1930. *H. G. W. Household*

The line continued to exist, in a more or less derelict state, for the next 30 years or so.

In 1889, the 'main line' as far as Longdon Road, together with the branch to Shipston, was reconstructed on the standard gauge and to allow the use of locomotives — the line being described as a 'Steam Tramway'. The new line was just over nine miles long, with intermediate stations at Stretton-on-Fosse and Longdon Road which were of the simplest construction, with single platform and one short siding. At Shipston-on-Stour there was also a single platform, but with a loop for 'running round', a goods shed, and a small engine shed. All signals on the branch were worked from ground frames.

At the time of opening in 1889, an ancient 0-6-0ST, No 47, which had begun life as a tender engine on the Shrewsbury & Birmingham Railway in 1849, worked the line. When this was withdrawn from service a few months later, its place was taken by one of the little '850' or '1901' class 0-6-0STs, No 2015 was at Shipston in 1901. The track being of light construction, there were severe limits on the engines which were allowed. The shed at Shipston was closed in November 1916, though the only facility at Moreton was an engine siding.

In 1902, the service consisted of four trains in each direction two each way being mixed. The first train left Shipston at 6.50am, and arrived at Moreton at 7.35am. The 11.05am was mixed, as was the 3.25pm and the last train was at 6.55pm. From Moreton, trains left at 9.20am mixed, 1.20pm, 5.05pm mixed and 8.15pm. There was no service on Sundays. The passenger service was withdrawn as from 8 July 1929, but the line remained open for goods traffic.

By the late 1930s there were no working signals,

**87**
The heaviest engines allowed over the Banbury & Cheltenham Direct line were the '2800' class 2-8-0s. No 2872, on a train of Baldwin's wagons loaded with iron ore from Hook Norton for South Wales, waits for signals at Charlton Kings. 7 June 1923.
*H. G. W. Household*

**88**
'Metro' 2-4-0T No 3563 on a Leamington train at Stratford-on-Avon in 1928. Built in 1894, No 3563 was later rebuilt with larger tanks and remained in service until December 1944.
*LGRP, courtesy David & Charles*

**89**
'517' class 0-4-2T No 526 in charge of a Winchcombe to Cheltenham local train near Cheltenham Racecourse, 24 July 1924. One of the first engines of the class, and originally a saddle tank, No 526 was built at Wolverhampton in 1868 and was withdrawn from service in September 1933.   *H. G. W. Household*

while the gates to the six level crossings were devoid of any locking devices! The GWR Working Time Table still referred to the line as a 'Tramway'. The time allowed for the daily goods workings gave a speed of approx $5\frac{1}{2}$mph! As from 1 June 1941, both Stretton and London Road were closed to all traffic; however, the line outlived the GWR and was not finally closed until May 1960.

### Honeybourne and Stratford-on-Avon

This was the second branch to be opened by the OW&WR, the opening taking place on 11 July, 1859. Like the branch to Chipping Norton it was destined to become part of a through route to Cheltenham, though this was not to happen for nearly half a century. What did take place within a short period of time was the extension of the line to meet the GWR's branch from Hatton, this happening in 1861 and resulting in the introduction of through trains between Leamington and Worcester (and, at first, Malvern).

The original branch was $9\frac{1}{2}$ miles long, of single track, and had two intermediate stations, at Long Marston and Milcote. A third section was opened at Broad Marston in October 1904, but this was closed in July 1916. Pebworth was opened between Honey-

bourne and what had been the site of Broad Marston in September 1937.

The first engines to work the branch must have been tender engines, as the Company possessed only two passenger tank engines — 'Mr and Mrs Johnson' which were employed on the Chipping Norton branch and between Henwick and Malvern. From 1861 the branch was worked by No 68 (GWR No 225), a Beyer, Peacock 2-4-0T. With its sister engine, No 69, which worked between Worcester and Malvern, it inaugurated the through service to and from Leamington. Both these engines were withdrawn by the early 1880s, their place being taken by the '517' class 0-4-2Ts. In 1901, No 1431 was shedded at the small engine shed situated to the south of the old station at Stratford. There was also a shed at Honeybourne, but at that time this housed only two 0-6-0STs, Nos 650 and 1775. Stratford-on-Avon shed was closed in 1910, when it was replaced by a large, new shed situated to the north of the station.

In 1902, there were seven trains in each direction between Honeybourne and Stratford. The first departure from Honeybourne was at 8.09am, this being the through train from Worcester to Birmingham, and this was followed at 9.16am by a through train from Evesham to Leamington. The 5.45pm was another through train from Worcester which ran to Leamington and eventually terminated at Oxford! Similarly, the early morning through train to Birmingham continued to Shrewsbury, while the final train of the day, leaving Honeybourne at 7.45pm, terminated at Wolverhampton at 10.25pm.

The first train from Stratford was at 8.27am, this being the 7.40am through train from Leamington to Worcester — which then continued via the Severn Valley line to Shrewsbury! The 10.35am originated as

**90**
Steam railmotor No 40 stands in Toddington station on the Cheltenham to Honeybourne service, 28 July 1910. *The late H. W. Household*

**91**
No 3825 *County of Devon* in charge of a Paignton to Wolverhampton train near Cheltenham Racecourse, 18 July 1924. For many years, the 'Counties' were the largest engines permitted to work over the LMS main line between Stabdish Junction and Yate. The first vehicle in the train is worthy of note!
*H. G. W. Household*

the 9.45am from Birmingham, non-stop to Stratford with TC for Honeybourne. The 11.35am was the 10.42am from Leamington to Worcester, while the 4.45pm to Honeybourne originated from Leamington. Finally, there was the 5.55pm Birmingham to Worcester, which left Stratford at 6.45pm. An additional late evening train ran from Stratford to Evesham on Fridays and Saturdays. There was no service on Sundays.

Among the many ambitious and expensive improvements which were carried out by the GWR in the early years of this century was the new line south-westwards from Honeybourne to Cheltenham — a proposal to be found among the original aims of the OW&WR — which provided a more direct route from Birmingham to South Wales and the West of England. As related in Chapter 3, this involved the complete reconstruction of Honeybourne station and the provision of new junctions. The first section was opened as far as Broadway

on 1 August 1904, and the whole line to Cheltenham came into use exactly two years later. The construction of this line owed not a little to the threat offered by a rival scheme — rather incredulously backed by the impecunious M&SWJR — the impetus for this being the desire of important agricultural interests to the south of Evesham for rail communication with city markets. During 1908 the doubling of the original branch line from Honeybourne to Stratford was completed.

In addition to the new services between Birmingham and Cardiff, and Wolverhampton and the West of England, a local service was commenced between Honeybourne and Cheltenham. This was one of many services on which the steam railcars were employed, and in later years auto-trains in charge of '517' class 0-4-2Ts took their place: both were worked from Cheltenham. This service was confined to the new line south of Honeybourne, the service to and from Stratford continued as in the past. By the 1930s the '5101' class 2-6-2Ts were in regular use, and a few years later diesel railcars took over some of the turns. The Cheltenham auto-trains had by this time been taken over by the '4800' class 0-4-2Ts.

In 1932, there were nine trains from Honeybourne to Stratford, with an additional late evening train on Saturdays; there were, however, only seven trains in the opposite direction, with an additional late evening one on Saturdays. The 8.05am from Honeybourne was a through train from Pershore to Snow Hill, and was followed at 8.31am by a through train from Worcester to Moor Street. The 11.07am went through to Leamington, as did the 2.03pm — the latter originating from Worcester. The 7.40am and 8.50am from Stratford were both through trains from Leamington to Honeybourne, while the 10.35am and 8.45pm were through trains from Leamington to Worcester. Finally, the 6.38pm was the familiar 5.55pm from Snow Hill to Worcester.

On the Honeybourne to Cheltenham line, the first train was the 6.48am auto-train from Cheltenham to Broadway and back, the first of three such workings. This was followed by the 7.30am to Honeybourne and back, there being five return trips each day — the last of which left Cheltenham at 6.25pm and Honeybourne at 7.52pm. One or two auto-trains filled in their waiting time to Honeybourne with a short working along the main line to Evesham and back, while there was also a return working between Honeybourne and Winchcombe by the engine and carriages of the 7.10am from Leamington Spa. The latter was one of two workings by ordinary stock, the other being the 5.08pm from Cheltenham which stopped only at the principal stations to Honeybourne (arr 5.57pm) and then worked to Moreton-in-Marsh and back (as related in Chapter 6) before returning from Honeybourne at 7.52pm — again calling only at the principal stations.

There was now a very limited service between Honeybourne and Stratford on Sundays; so limited that it consisted of an early morning train from Birmingham to Worcester, with a return working in the evening. Between Cheltenham and Honeybourne there were two return workings by auto-trains.

In 1947, there were 10 trains each way between Honeybourne and Stratford. The 7.15am was a through train from Evesham to Leamington, and the 8.11am was also a through train from Evesham — but to Snow Hill. This was followed by the 8.46am, the traditional morning train from Worcester to Moor Street. The 9.50am was the return working of a diesel railcar which had left Leamington earlier that

**92**

Hayles Abbey Halt, on the Honeybourne to Cheltenham line, was opened in 1928. 2-8-2T No 7214 heads south on a ballast train, September 1955. *R. C. Riley*

**93**

Closed to passengers in 1929, Shipston-on-Stour can rarely have seen so many people as on the occasion of the visit of a Rail Enthusiasts Club Special on 24 April 1953. The station building with its unusual panelled boards and deep awning was rather the worse for wear! *R. C. Riley*

morning. The 3.00pm was also a diesel railcar, being the 1.38pm from Worcester, which returned from Stratford at 4.00pm. The remaining trains were all local workings.

The first two trains from Stratford, at 8.05am and 8.48am were both diesel railcars from Leamington, and the 12.19am was the 11.32am from Leamington to Evesham. The 1.35pm also ran to Evesham, returning two hours later as a through train to Stratford. The 5.00pm was the only through train from Leamington (dep 4.20pm) to Worcester, and the 6.44pm was the traditional 5.55pm from Snow Hill to Worcester. The 7.20pm which terminated at Honeybourne was also a through train from Birmingham — and formed the early morning train from Evesham to Snow Hill. Only the 10.10am and 10.10pm were local trains from Stratford to Honeybourne. There were no trains on Sundays.

There were now only four auto-trains in each direction between Cheltenham and Honeybourne, the first

and last departures being very similar to those in 1932. There was still an early morning Cheltenham to Broadway return working, but the only other such working ran on Wednesdays, Thursdays and Saturdays only, leaving Cheltenham at 1.12pm and returning from Broadway at 2.30pm. The Cheltenham to Honeybourne and Moreton-in-Marsh return working now left at 4.40pm, and stopped at all stations, as did the return working which left Honeybourne at 7.23pm. The service on Sundays remained unaltered, with two auto-trains from Cheltenham to Honeybourne and back; however the morning train now left at 10.00am (9.35am in 1932) and did not return from Honeybourne until 1.45am (10.17am in 1932) as it ran to Worcester and back, this being the only through service of the week between Cheltenham and Worcester, and possibly the only such through train during the entire life of the West Midland Section.

# 9  Severn Valley and Welsh Marches

**The Severn Valley Railway**

The Severn Valley Railway was a major line, being almost 40 miles long, and was built to link the county towns of Worcestershire and Shropshire — both of which were situated on the Severn. It was opened from Hartlebury to Sutton Bridge Junction, Shrewsbury, on 1 February 1862, being worked by the WMR. Although following the course of the Severn, there were some fairly considerable gradients in places — such as from Stourport to Bewdley and north of Highley, where there was an ascent of 1 in 100 followed by a descent to Alveley Colliery. There were a number of wooden viaducts (later replaced by stone structures), only Bentle, north of Ironbridge, being of any great length — 203yd. There was also the Bridgnorth Tunnel, with a length of 559yds. The line was single throughout.

Considerable developments took place over the years at both Stourport and Buildwas. At the former, lines were laid to connect with the nearby Stafford & Worcester Canal and with the power station, while just north of the station what was known as the Burlish branch was opened in 1930 to serve industrial premises. At Buildwas, the opening of the Ironbridge power station in 1932 resulted in the provision of extensive coal sidings and a new signalbox. In addition to the traffic created by the new power stations, there was a considerable mineral traffic from Alveley Colliery, between Hampton to High Loade, the sidings there coming into use in 1939.

There were 13 intermediate stations between Hartlebury and Shrewsbury, to which four halts were added in the 1930s. Most stations had two platforms and a loop, though several originally had no loop and only a single platform. Stourport, Bewdley and Buildwas eventually had two signalboxes; however, at Bridgnorth the original two signalboxes were later replaced by one new box.

Originally the train service provided several through trains in each direction between Worcester and Shrewsbury. However, the opening of the line from Kidderminster to Bewdley in 1878 eventually brought about the diversion of most trains to run to and from Kidderminster. Others ran to and from Hartlebury or Bewdley, with some local trains to Bridgnorth and back, while in later year the section between Kidderminster and Bewdley had a 'shuttle' service provided mostly by a diesel railcar.

As with all the former WMR lines, the Severn Valley saw a gradual replacement of the original Company's engine by those of the GWR — though in one or two cases not of GWR origin. Nos 106 and 107 were 2-4-0s which had been built in 1854 by Fairbairn's for the Birkenhead Railway and rebuilt at Wolverhampton in the 1870s; they spent a number of years working from Shrewsbury to Worcester until withdrawn in 1900 and 1902. Two very different 2-4-0s also employed on those duties were Nos 150 and 151 of the 'Chancellor' class, which finished their lives on the line, being withdrawn in 1918 and 1920. Among ex-WMR engines used were Nos 192 and 193, from the old NA&HR, which were withdrawn in 1902-3.

In 1902, there were five trains from Hartlebury to Shrewsbury, the first two morning trains being from Worcester (dep 7.20am and 9.45am) — the second of which originated from Leamington. There were also two trains from Worcester to Bridgnorth, the 7.43pm being via Kidderminster. Between Hartlebury and Bewdley there were a couple of local trains, and there was an evening train from Bridgnorth to Shrewsbury — with another from Ironbridge on Saturdays only.

In the opposite direction, the first train was the 7.35am from Bridgnorth to Worcester. There were two trains from Shrewsbury to Worcester, two between Shrewsbury and Hartlebury, and a fifth which ran to Kidderminster. The 7.43pm from Worcester to Bridgnorth returned to Kidderminster. The only other

trains were a couple of locals between Bewdley and Hartlebury. There were no trains on Sundays.

Thirty years later, in 1932, there had been some considerable changes. Only two trains ran from Hartlebury to Shrewsbury, one being the 7.05am from Worcester, but there were three from Kidderminster. Auto-trains ran between Hartlebury, Bewdley and Bridgnorth, though a couple only ran as far as Highley and back. From Shrewsbury, there were four trains to Kidderminster and one to Hartlebury. There were also the return workings of the auto-trains from Bridgnorth. Most surprising was the existence of a a service on Sundays, albeit that this consisted of the 7.30am from Birmingham, which left Kidderminster at 8.30am and arrived at Shrewsbury at 10.30am, and a return working leaving Shrewsbury at 5.50pm, arriving at Birmingham at 8.46pm.

Considerable changes had also taken place as far as motive power was concerned, with the disappearance of the older tender engines. The small '4500' class 2-6-2Ts were to be found on the passenger services and, at a later date, some of the local workings were by diesel railcars. Coal traffic from Alveley Colliery was handled by the '4300' class 2-6-0s, a couple of which were shedded at Kidderminster and which worked tender-first to the colliery on empty wagon trains; while between Shrewsbury and Buildwas, 'Hall' class 4-6-0s were to be found on coal trains for the power station.

By 1947, the service had been reduced to four trains in each direction. The first train to Shrewsbury was still a through train from Worcester (dep 6.55am) and

**94**
Stourport station at the beginning of this century. In later years, Stourport's importance increased considerably as a result of the building of a power station nearby, and it enjoyed a frequent service of auto-trains or diesel railcars. *K. Beddoes Collection*

**95**
Arley station c1906. As at many country stations, the Station Master's house was the most imposing section of the premises. *Barry Geens per W. Smith*

there were two trains from Hartlebury and one from Kidderminster. However, only one train from Shrewsbury went to Hartlebury, the other three being to Kidderminster! One of the latter made a prolonged stop at Bridgnorth from 2.08pm to 3.05pm. There was an afternoon return working by a diesel railcar between Kidderminster and Bridgnorth, also an evening return working by one between Hartlebury and Buildwas — the return working terminating at Worcester. The remaining trains were two diesel railcar workings to Highley and back, from Kidderminster and Bewdley respectively. On the northern section, there were return workings by two local trains between Shrewsbury and Bridgnorth and Buildwas respectively. Finally, except on Saturdays, there was an early morning diesel railcar from Highley (dep

6.07am) to Kidderminster. There was no service on Sundays.

## The Tenbury & Bewdley Railway

Bewdley developed into an important junction during the later part of the last century, though it was not unitl the inter-war years that the maximum flow of traffic was reached. The first stage in this development took place within a couple of years of the opening of the SVR, when the Tenbury & Bewdley Railway was opened on 13 August 1864. Just over 15 miles long, the line ran from a junction with the SVR at Bewdley to the little town of Tenbury Wells which was already the terminus of the Tenbury Railway's branch from Woofferton. Although a few trains continued to run between Woofferton and Tenbury, the two lines were integrated as one long branch. The last, and in many ways the most important line, was not opened until 1 June 1878, when the three miles between Kidderminster Junction and Bewdley came into use. This not only made possible a through service between Kidderminster and Woofferton (including, at one time, the running of TC between Woofferton and Birmingham and Wolverhampton), but brought about the gradual transfer of the SVR services from Hartlebury and Worcester to Kidderminster.

Both sections of line were single track, and the line from Bewdley to Tenbury was quite heavily graded and severely curved for the first few miles through the Wyre Forest to Cleobury Mortimer. The short section between Kidderminster and Bewdley included Bewdley Tunnel (486yd long), which was followed almost

immediately by the Sandbourne Viaduct — shared by the SVR. Later improvements at Bewdley included the provision of a run-round loop behind the island platform. There were four intermediate stations between Bewdley and Tenbury, of which only Cleobury Mortimer had two platforms. The layout at the latter station was altered and extended when the Cleobury Mortimer & Ditton Priors Light Railway was opened in 1908. A second platform was also provided at a later date at Neen Sollars and a loop added to the line at Newnham Bridge.

At Tenbury Wells the station had two platforms, several goods sidings and, in earlier years, a turntable. The only station between Tenbury Wells and Woofferton, at Easton Court, had a single platform and goods siding. There were originally signalboxes at each of the stations between Bewdley and Tenbury, but that at Newnham Bridge was later replaced by three ground frames. At Tenbury Wells there were originally two boxes, the West Box which was closed in the 1920s being that for the Tenbury Railway. A single ground frame sufficed at Easton Court.

At the far end of the line, Woofferton had a bay behind the Shrewsbury platform and there had originally been an engine shed for the use of the Tenbury Railway engine. However, this was out of use by 1896, though it was used as a stabling and water point for many years afterwards. After closure, the engine was provided initially by Leominster, but in later years the engine spent the night at Ludlow.

Although there was little scope for the development of the line by the opening of extra stations or halts, two

of the latter were opened between Kidderminster and Bewdley, these being Foley Park Halt and Rifle Range Halt — both opened in 1905, when steam railmotors were introduced between Kidderminster and Bewdley. The latter halt did not have a long life, being dependent for traffic on the use of the local rifle range which was closed before 1932; however, Foley Park survived to the end of the GWR and in later days had several sidings for traffic to and from the Sugar Beet Factory.

A variety of engines, both tender and tank, worked over the line, though traffic on the western section did not tend to be very heavy, as in 1929 when a Beyer, Peacock double-framed 0-6-0 running tender-first on a single carriage constituted the train! The '517' class 0-4-2Ts of earlier days gave place to the '4500' class 2-6-2Ts, and various 0-6-0STs and 0-6-0PTs, were used for the goods workings — as were the '4500' class. In later days a diesel railcar covered most of the passenger duties, especially the frequent 'shuttle' service between Kidderminster, Bewdley and Hartlebury — though auto-trains had been used on the latter service in earlier years.

During the war years, 1939-45, considerable traffic in ammunition was carried to and from Cleobury Mortimer Junction. LNER 'J25' class and 'Dean Goods' 0-6-0s, 'Aberdare' class 2-6-0s, and even an occasional '2800' class 2-8-0, appeared on these trains, while on one occasion 'Bulldog' class 4-4-0 No 3393 *Australia* was observed.

In 1902, there were five trains in each direction between Kidderminster and Woofferton. The first train left Kidderminster at 8.40am (being 'Mixed' between Tenbury and Woofferton), and the last was at 7.08pm.

**96**
Steam at Bridgnorth, in the shape of a 1904 Clarkson 20hp steam bus (DA 81) standing outside the station. Unlike in other areas, the GWR bus services in the Severn Valley did not remain railway-operated for many years. *Real Photos*

**97**
Buildwas station served only a small village, but was the junction for lines to Much Wenlock and Craven Arms, Wellington, and Shifnal. The single platform at the higher level was used by the Much Wenlock and Craven Arms trains. No 4104 is in charge of the 8.15am Shrewsbury-Kidderminster service. *R. C. Riley*

The 5.39pm train had TC from Birmingham to Woofferton. The first train from Woofferton was at 7.07am this having TC for Wolverhampton, while the last train left for Kidderminster at 4.30pm! There were also three local workings between Woofferton and Tenbury Wells, the 5.30pm being another 'mixed' train. Apart from through trains to Woofferton or the SVR there were only a couple of trains between Kidderminster and Bewdley. There were no trains on Sundays.

There were still five trains each way in 1932, the first from Kidderminster being at 8.48am, while the last now left at 6.00pm. Both 'mixed' trains and

through carriages had disappeared from the Time Tables. On Thursdays and Saturdays there was an additional evening train to Tenbury and back. The first train from Woofferton was now at 8.30am and the last at 6.48pm — over two hours later than in 1902. Three trains ran in each direction between Woofferton and Tenbury — two being to and from Ludlow — and another two ran on Saturdays Only. There was still no service on Sundays. Between Kidderminster and Bewdley there were now more than 30 trains in each direction(!), though some ran only on Saturdays, and a number were auto-trains. There were also four trains each way on Sundays, three of which ran to and from Stourport.

By 1947, the service had largely been taken over by a diesel railcar, three of the five workings in each direction being so covered. The vehicle spent the night at Ludlow. The first train (of ordinary stock) left Kidderminster at 8.50am and the last (a diesel railcar) at 6.25pm. The first train from Woofferton was the 8.09am. Diesel railcar (7.52am from Ludlow), while the last train was not until 7.55pm — three and a half hours later than in 1902! This was the return working of the 4.38pm from Kidderminster, of ordinary stock. Once again, there was no service on Sundays.

There were also three return workings by auto-trains between Woofferton and Tenbury. One duty commenced with the 7.25am from Leominster and did two return trips on the branch before returning to Leominster at 8.56am. The other duty commenced with the 3.25pm Leominster to Ludlow, continued with the 4.23pm Ludlow to Tenbury, and concluded at Woofferton at 4.56pm.

The prewar summer service of 30 trains between Kidderminster and Bewdley had been reduced to about half that number in the winter of 1947, though there were now eight trains each way between Bewdley and Hartlebury — reflecting the growth of Stourport. A considerable number of these turns were worked by a diesel railcar. On Sundays there was a return working between Kidderminster and Stourport in the morning, while in the evening there was the 6.05pm from Hartlebury to Birmingham via Bewdley.

**The Much Wenlock Railway**

Simultaneously with the opening of the SVR on 1 February 1862, there took place the opening of the short branch — $3\frac{1}{2}$ miles long — from Buildwas to Much Wenlock, this being the Much Wenlock & Severn Junction Railway, which was worked by the WMR.

A branch line from Madeley Junction, between Wellington and Shifnal, through Madeley to Lightmoor, had been opened by the Shrewsbury & Birmingham Railway in 1854; while on 1 July 1861, the GWR took over the working of the Wellington & Severn Junction Railway, from Ketley Junction to Lightmoor, which had been built in 1857 and worked by the Coalbrookdale Iron Co. A new line was built southward form Lightmoor by the GWR as far as Coalbrookdale, and at the same time the Much Wenlock Railway built a line to Coalbrookdale from Buildwas, a distance of just over two miles — but which included the Royal Albert Bridge over the Severn. The link was established on 1 November 1864. Both the Lightmoor to Coalbrookdale and the

Buildwas to Coalbrookdale lines were double track, including the Royal Albert Bridge, but the other lines were all single track.

A few weeks later, on 5 December a further section of the Wenlock Railway was opened, this being westwards from Much Wenlock to Presthope, a distance of a little under three miles. Just over three years later, on 16 December 1867, the final section of the Wenlock Railway, the 11 miles from Presthope to Marsh Farm Junction, to the north of Craven Arms, was opened to traffic.

The extension from Much Wenlock to Presthope had involved the bypassing of the original station, the new station being sited nearer to Buildwas: however, the old premises continued in use as the goods station and as the site of the small engine shed. All the stations, at Presthope, Longville, Rushbury and Harton Road, had only one platform — as had Much Wenlock — and apart from Presthope the provision for goods traffic was limited. There was a passing loop at Presthope and shorter loops at the other stations; though that at Harton Road was used for 'running-round' in the 1930s. Much Wenlock and Presthope had signalboxes, and one was provided at Rushbury in later years. Three halts were opened in mid-1930s in a rather forlorn attempt to increase passenger traffic.

For many years the engines working over the Wellington to Craven Arms line were either Wolverhampton-built 0-6-0STs or the usual little '517' class 0-4-2Ts. However, in 1935 the small 2-6-2Ts of the '4400' class, with 4ft $1\frac{1}{2}$in wheels, arrived at Wellington for this work, and five of the 11 engines in the class were so employed for the remainder of the GWR's existence. In 1938, one of these engines shared the small sub-shed at Much Wenlock with an 0-6-0PT, but in 1947 the allocation was two '4400' class engines, Nos 4401 and 4409. At one period,

**98**

Small-wheeled 2-6-2T No 4409 nears Much Wenlock on a train from Craven Arms to Wellington. For many years five engines of this class were at Wellington, or at the small sub-shed at Much Wenlock, especially for this line. *H. C. Casserley*

**99**

The stone-built goods shed at Much Wenlock was a most attractive building. The track at the bottom left-hand corner formerly led to the small engine shed which closed in 1951. *R. S. Carpenter*

**100**

Traffic on the Tenbury & Bewdley Railway rarely warranted more than one or two carriages, at least in later years when diesel railcars worked much of the service. An ex-GWR Railcar leaves Newnham Bridge for Bewdley in 1956. *W. Smith collection*

steam railcars were also used between Much Wenlock and Craven Arms.

West of Much Wenlock, both the service and the amount of traffic was very much less than between Much Wenlock and Wellington. In 1902, there was only one train between Wellington and Craven Arms, and this did not leave until 4.30pm! The only other trains to Craven Arms were the 6.25am mixed from Much Wenlock and the 9.30am from Shifnal via Madeley. The 3.05pm from Wellington went as far as Presthope, and there were three trains from Wellington to Much Wenlock, the 9.10pm being mixed from Buildwas. There was also the 4.05pm from Shifnal to

Much Wenlock, which was followed by the 5.18pm from Wolverhampton to Wenlock; the latter returned as the 7.20pm to Buildwas and Shrewsbury.

There were two trains from Craven Arms to Wellington, at 8.15am and 6.38pm, and there was the 11.40 mixed train to Much Wenlock (arr 1.05pm), except on Mondays when it ran as an ordinary passenger train leaving at 11.35am and arriving at Wenlock at 12.23pm. Two trains ran from Much Wenlock to Wellington, at 7.30am and 1.45pm and there was the 4.15pm from Presthope to Wellington. The only other trains were the 2.50pm to Shifnal (returning from Shifnal at 4.05pm) and the 7.20pm from Much Wenlock to Buildwas and Shrewsbury. Although it might not have been expected, there was a service of one train in each direction between Wellington and Much Wenlock on Sundays, leaving Wellington at 9.35am and returning from Much Wenlock at 6.55pm.

Thirty years later, in 1932, there were considerable differences not least because passenger trains no longer ran over the Shifnal to Lightmoor line. There were now two trains from Wellington to Craven Arms, at 8.17am and 3.00pm, as well as the early morning train from Much Wenlock (dep 6.30am). There was no longer a Wellington to Presthope working, this having been replaced by the 5.25pm to Horton Road. Four trains ran between Wellington and Much Wenlock, with an additional late evening train at 10.25pm on Saturdays Only.

Three trains now ran from Craven Arms to Wellington, at 7.50am, 11.05am and 4.50pm, and there was also the 7.05pm from Harton Road. Another four

99

100

101

102

103

**101**
Tenbury Wells was originally the terminus of a short branch line from Woofferton, but became a through station when the line from Bewdley was opened in 1864. The abrupt change of gradient should be noticed! *W. Smith collection*

**102**
Ex-CMDP 0-6-0PT No 29 shunting at Ditton Priors on 30 March, 1938, a few months before the passenger service was withdrawn from the Cleobury Mortimer & Ditton Priors line. Four-wheeled carriages survived to the end of the service. *R. S. Carpenter*

**103**
Kington was the most important station on the branch line that ran westwards from Leominster to New Radnor. Goods traffic was dealt with at the original terminus which was by-passed when the line was extended to New Radnor in 1875. July 1951. *R. C. Riley*

trains ran from Much Wenlock to Wellington, with a fifth (at 8.00pm) on Saturdays Only. However, there were now no trains on Sundays.

In 1947, there were still only two Wellington to Craven Arms trains, running at the same times as in 1932, while the early morning train from Much Wenlock was still leaving at 6.30am. However, there were no longer any other trains west of Much Wenlock, as the remaining five trains all terminated there, with an additional 10.00pm train on Saturdays Only. There was also a Saturdays Only train from Ketley to Much Wenlock, at 12.45pm. The three trains from Craven Arms ran at very much the same time as in 1932, but there were only two from Much Wenlock to Wellington — the evening train running an hour later on Saturdays — though a couple of trains ran between Buildwas and Wellington. Once again, there was no service on Sundays.

**The Leominster Branches**
On 1 July 1862, the WMR took over the working of the $13\frac{1}{2}$ miles of the Leominster & Kington Railway, which had been opened on 2 August 1857, and worked by the Contractor, Brassey, in fairly close association with the S&HR. The line was actually taken over jointly with the GWR, passing into the sole ownership of the latter after 1864.

The single track ran from Kington Junction, to the north of Leominster, through the western parts of Herefordshire to the small town of Kington, with inter-mediate stations at Kingsland, Pembridge and Titley, none of which served any community of more than a few hundred people. Consequently, argicultural traffic was of more consequence than passengers as far as the revenues were concerned. The largest station was the terminus at Kington. For the first few years the line was worked by two Crewe type 2-4-0WTs owned by the Company (later GWR Nos 229 and 230), and which were shedded in the S&HR shed at Leominster.

Despite the small population of the area, it was considered large enough to warrant the construction of no less than three additional lines! With the Kington branch these ultimately formed an integrated system. The first of these new lines was the Kington & Eardisley Railway, which ran south-westwards from Titley to a junction with the MR's line to Brecon at Eardisley, a distance of just under eight miles. This was opened on 3 August 1874, with stations at Lyonshall and Almeley — the MR station being used at Eardisley. The service ran to and from Kington.

The following year the two remaining lines were opened, both in September. A branch of the Leominster & Kington was opened from Titley to Presteign, a distance of just over five and a half miles, on 10 September; while on the 25th, an extension from Kington was opened over the border into Radnorshire to the little town of New Radnor. This extension, $6\frac{1}{2}$ miles long, was not part of the Leominster & Kington, as might have been expected, but constituted a detached part of the Kington & Eardisley!

At the same time as these two lines were opened, a small engine shed came into use at Kington. This was built about 100yd to the west of the new station, the line to New Radnor having been constructed a little to the north of the old station which remained in use as a goods station. Witney, Chipping Norton, Much Wenlock, Kington — there seems to have been an epidemic of bypassing original stations when extending branches! The new station at Kington had two platforms and a passing loop. Signalboxes were provided for all the original stations on the L&KR — and one was provided at the new station at Kington — but Presteign and stations on both sections of the K&ER had only ground frames.

The original Crewe type tank engines had been replaced before the new lines were opened, and the first occupants of the new shed at Kington would have been a couple of the '517' class 0-4-2Ts. These engines worked on all three lines for the next 60 years or so, particularly No 202 which practically lived on the branch for years on end before being withdrawn in 1928. The usual 0-6-0STs dealt with goods traffic.

In 1902, there were three trains in each direction between Leominster and New Radnor, with an additional train on Saturday evenings from Leominster which returned only as far as Kington. The first train

**104, 105**
Presteign's station building was quite impressive, though hardly justified by the amount of traffic and paucity of train services.  *Both: Ian Allan Library*

**106**
Lyonshall station in 1932, a typical rural station in the remote parts of the Welsh Marches. The Kington-Eardisley line was closed to all traffic in 1940. *LGRP, courtesy David & Charles*

104

105

102

106

left Leominster at 9.55am, there was a mixed train at 1.00pm and the last departure was at 4.05pm. None of the return workings from New Radnor was mixed. There were also three trains from Leominster to Kington, the first being a mixed at 5.30am and the last left at 8.45pm — this being extended to New Radnor on Saturdays. There were only two trains from Kington to Leominster, the imbalance in the service being due to the first train each day commencing from Leominster, while the last train terminated at Kington. Although it might not have been expected, there was a service on Sundays, consisting of two trains in each direction between Leominster and Kington; from Leominster, the usual 5.30am mixed and the 6.40pm, and from Kington there were the 8.00am and 7.45pm.

The Eardisley and Presteign branch services were integrated, so that one engine and set of carriages would cover all the workings. Both services ran to and from Kington, consequently the section between Kington and Titley had no less than 14 trains each way on weekdays! The workings began with the 6.50am from Kington to Presteign and return, followed by the 9.10am to Eardisley and back. There were four such workings over each branch, the last to Presteign being at 5.05pm, except on Mondays and Saturdays when there was an extra train at 6.30pm, returning from Presteign at 7.10pm. This additional working necessitated the provision of an extra engine and set of carriages, as the last train from Kington to Eardisley departed at 6.15pm, returning from Eardisley at 7.10pm.

This meant that on those evenings Kington had up trains departing at 6.12pm (Leominster), 6.25pm (Eardisley) and 6.30pm (Presteign), while the 5.30pm from Leominster arrived at 6.23pm. The 3.25pm to Eardisley and the 1.20pm to Presteign were mixed, as were the midday from Eardisley and the 2.25pm from Presteign. There were no Sunday trains on either branch.

In the summer of 1932, there were still three trains each way between Leominster and New Radnor, with another three between Leominster and Kington; though there was no longer a late evening train to New Radnor on Saturdays. The times were very similar to those in 1902; however, the last train to New Radnor now left at 5.00pm instead of 4.05pm, while the first train to Kington was not until 6.18am. An additional train ran from Kington to Leominster at 1.40pm. There were no trains on Sundays.

Both the Presteign and Eardisley branches had been reduced to three trains each way: as the early morning train to Presteign and back had been withdrawn, the first train now left Kington at 10.25am. On the Eardisley branch, the first train was at 9.00am and it was the evening trains which had been withdrawn, the last now leaving Kington at 3.30pm and returning from Eardisley at 4.48pm. This reduction reflected the growth of local bus services in the rural areas.

The withdrawl of the old '517' class engines brought the appearance of the new '4800' class 0-4-2Ts, these being of the non-auto 58xx series, several of which were shared between Leominster and Kington. During

103

the war years both sheds were transferred to be under Hereford, having previously been sub-sheds of Worcester.

The line to Eardisley was closed to all traffic in 1940, and did not even appear on the GWR map in 1947; though the Time Tables gave the optimistic information 'Service Suspended'. There were only two trains each way between Leominster and New Radnor, though there were still three between Leominster and Kington. The times remained much as they had been in 1902! The Presteign branch service had been further reduced to only two trains in each direction, with a third on Saturdays.

### The Worcester, Bromyard & Leominster Railway

As related in Chapter 3, few lines had a more protracted period of construction than this cross-country branch. The 24 miles of line took almost as many years to construct! Opened as far as Yearsett, seven miles, on 22 May, 1874, the line was extended a further four miles to Bromyard on 22 May 1877, resulting in the closure of Yearsett station. However, in this case no new station was provided on the extension line, Yearsett disappearing for ever from the Time Tables. It probably enjoyed the distinction of being the GWR station to have the shortest life!

Intermediate stations on the single line branch were provided at Ligh Court, Knightwick and Suckley, the two former having signalboxes — though Knigh-

**107**
Almeley station served a very rural community, as is evident by its lack of facilities. 1932.
*LGRP, courtesy David & Charles*

**108**
Typical of the Golden Valley line, Westbrook station with a '517' class 0-4-2T on the branch train in 1932.
*LGRP, courtesy David & Charles*

twick's was closed from 1922-1947, but not demolished. There were two short viaducts between Leigh Court and Knightwick, at Hayley Dingle and Broad Dingle. The terminus at Bromyard had a single platform, signalbox, several sidings and a goods shed, also a small engine shed.

The next stage was the opening of not quite four miles at the western end, from Leominster to Steens Bridge, on 1 March 1884. The simple terminus at Steens Bridge had only one platform, with run-round loop and two short sidings, no signalbox being provided. The two sections remained isolated for the next 13 years. Finally, on 1 September 1897, the intervening nine miles were opened and Leominster was, at long last, linked to Worcester. The extension involved considerable alterations at Bromyard, though the original premises did remain as part of the enlarged station which now had two platforms. The small engine shed, now being redundant, was closed and pulled down. Two stations were provided on the new section, at Fencote and Rowden Mill. The former had two platforms, a crossing loop and signalbox; but Rowden Mill had just a single platform.

To the east of Bromyard, Suckley station was extended and enlarged early in this century, when a crossing loop and a second platform were provided, with a signalbox to replace the ground frames.

Apart from Bromyard, there were few communities of any size served by the line, so that passenger traffic was never very heavy. The line was worked by the usual '517' class 0-4-2Ts, with 0-6-0STs on the goods trains. Both Worcester and Leominster sub-shed (transferred to be under Worcester) provided engines for the line, as the pattern of services over the years required this — there were early morning trains from both Worcester and Leominster, with a similar provision of trains in the evening.

In 1902, there were five trains in each direction, the evening train from Leominster (dep 7.45pm) waiting at Bromyard to cross the last evening train from Worcester (dep 7.55pm). The first trains in the morning were at 7.20pm from Leominster and 8.20am from Worcester, which passed each other between Henwick and Foregate Street. There was no service on Sundays. Thirty years later, in the summer of 1932, there were still five trains each way, with a sixth from Worcester to Bromyard and back. Three trains now

ran between Worcester and Bromyard on Sundays, the first leaving Worcester at 9.40am and the last at 5.50pm. Stoke Prior Halt had been opened between Leominster and Steens Bridge in July 1929.

There were few changes, apart from the provision of slightly more modern engines and carriages, during the remainder of the GWR's life; though a diesel railcar was used on some workings. For the most part, the '58xx' non-auto 0-4-2Ts took over the passenger trains; however, a couple of the last Wolverhampton-built 0-4-2Ts of the '3571' class were also used in the 1930s and No 3574 remained on these duties until withdrawn in 1949. Similarly, although one of the modern '7400' class 0-6-0PTs was used on freight workings, the older Dean pannier tanks were also still used.

In 1947, there were still five trains in each direction, and still at times very similar to those in 1902! The last train from Leominster, at 7.45pm, was a diesel railcar: however, how it reached Leominster was not evident from the Time Tables. There were also additional trains between Worcester and Bromyard on Thursdays and Saturdays, and an early evening return working by a diesel railcar which left Worcester at 5.40pm.

As with a number of other branch lines, it is doubtful if the receipts ever justified its construction and it was doomed from the time when the first rural bus services were commenced; though, like many similar lines — and indeed the GWR itself — it took a long time to die.

108

# Appendix A
## West Midland Engine Sheds

**Oxford, Worcester & Wolverhampton Railway.**
*Oxford:* Four road terminal shed, wooden construction. Repair shop. Opened in 1852. Layout considerably modified in this century. In use 1947.
*Worcester:* Four road terminal shed (Goods) and three road through shed (Passenger), both of brick. Opened in 1852. In use 1947.
*Kidderminster:* Single road terminal shed (later converted to through shed), wooden construction. Closed and replaced in 1932*.
*Dudley:* Single road, long wooden building. Opened in 1854, closed in 1870.
*Wolverhampton (Joint Station):* Three road terminal shed, wooden construction. Opened in 1854, closed c1864.
*Chipping Norton:* Single road through shed, stone and brick. Opened in 1855. Closed in 1922.
*Honeybourne:* Single road, brick. Opened c1853. Removed to new site in 1907, later burnt down. Closed in 1911.
*Evesham:* Single road terminal shed, timber walls (but built partly under road bridge). Opened c1853. Closed and replaced in 1901*.
*Stratford-on-Avon:* Single road, timber sides on dwarf brick walls. Opened in 1859. Closed and replaced in 1910*.

**Newport, Abergavenny & Hereford Railway**
*Hereford (Barton):* Eight roads, terminal building of stone, with roof pitches transverse to tracks. Repair shops at rear. Opened in 1853. Considerable alterations to yard layout, etc in this century. In use 1947.
*Abergavenny:* Single road, through shed, stone built. Opened in 1854. Closed 1932.

**Shrewsbury & Hereford Railway**
*Shrewsbury (Coleham):* Three roads, terminal shed. Repair shops adjacent. Opened in 1852. Greatly enlarged and layout altered over many years. In use in 1947.
*Leominster:* Two road, terminal shed, brick construction. Opened in 1853, closed in 1901*.
*Ludlow:* Single road, terminal shed, brick construction. Opened c1857. In use 1947.
*Woofferton:* Single road, brick built. Opened 1861, closed by 1896.
*Hereford (Barr's Court):* Three road terminal shed, stone built. Opened in 1852. Used only by LNWR (later LMS). Closed in 1935.

**Worcester & Hereford Railway**
Malvern Wells: Single road, brick construction. Opened in 1860. Closed and replaced in 1901*.

**West Midland Railway:**
*Witney:* Single road, stone construction. Opened in 1861. Closed in 1873.
*Much Wenlock:* Single road terminal shed, brick construction. Opened in 1861. In use 1947.

The GWR replaced Dudley with a shed at *Stourbridge Junction* in 1870. The shed was closed in 1926, when a new shed was built nearby, but remained in use for Rail Motors (later diesel railcars) and was re-opened to locomotives in 1944. Still in use 1947. A new shed on a different site was opened at *Kidderminster* in 1932, in use 1947. Smaller sheds were opened by the GWR as follows: *Bromyard:* Opened in 1877, closed in 1897. *Chipping Norton Junction:* Opened in 1881, demolished in 1907: replaced by new shed (Kingham) in 1913 — latter in use in 1947. *Fairford:* Opened 1873, still in use 1947. *Shipston-on-Stour:* Opened 1889, closed in 1916.

* Replacement sheds were also opened — *Leominster* opened in 1901, in use 1947. *Malvern Wells* opened in

**109**

Worcester shed in 1894. The majority of engines visible are either saddle tanks (of at least three different varieties) or 0-6-0s of the 'Dean Goods' and 'Standard Goods' classes, though there is also a solitary '517' class 0-4-2T. *LGRP, courtesy David & Charles*

**110**

Worcester shed in 1949, with 0-6-0PTs Nos 4641 and 2799. Unlike the majority of GWR sheds, Worcester was never provided with a ramped coaling stage. A crane and buckets were the only aids provided until 1944 when a small hoist was added. *Author*

**111**

The shed yard at Worcester was intersected by a line leading to the local coal depot and the Vinegar Branch. No 2007, one of the two remaining '1901' class saddle tanks, was the regular engine for shunting the coal yard. 15 June 1949. *Author*

110

111

1901. Closed in 1922. Evesham opened in 1901, in use 1947.

Engine sidings and servicing facilities existed at *Ledbury* from c1861 and at *Hartlebury* and *Moreton-in-Marsh*. At *Honeybourne* similar provision existed after the shed was burnt down and not replaced.

At *Stratford-on-Avon* the replacement shed was north of the station and outside the WMR section. Two road building , opened in 1910. In use 1947.

# Appendix B
## Allocation of Locomotives — Worcester, Hereford, Kidderminster and Stourbridge, January 1938 and December 1947

**Worcester 1938**

4-6-0 (13)
  'Castle'      5042/9/50/63
  'Star'      4049/51
  'Hall'      4958, 5914/42/5/56
  'Grange'      6807/51

4-4-0 (4)
  'Bulldog'      3353/89, 3418
  '32xx'      3209

2-8-0 (3)
  '28xx'      2850
  'ROD'      3007/27

2-6-0 (8)
  '26xx'      2613
  '43xx'      4367/32, 5312, 6306/24/82, 7301

0-6-0 (20)
  '2301'      2339/75/80, 2400/3/22/58, 2515/7/9/39/41/8/51/7/77
  '2251'      2263/74/8/83

2-6-2T (9)
  '45xx'      4546/58
  '4575'      4575, 5527
  '5101'      4100/14, 5173
  '51xx'      5114/33

0-6-0T (15)
  '850'      1220, 1919, 2016/9
  '2021'      2051, 2121/57
  '655'      1741
  '1854'      1798, 1898
  '1813'      1839
  '2721'      2743/99
  '57xx'      3728, 7750

0-4-2T (9)
  '3571'      3573/4
  '48xx'      4804/18, 5807/8/14/5/7

*Total 81*

Diesel railcars (3) 5, 6, 7
Sub sheds:
  Evesham      One '23xx', one '45xx'
  Honeybourne    One '23xx'
  Kington      Two 0-4-2T ('58xx')
  Leominster    Two 0-4-2T ('58xx'), one 0-6-0PT

**Worcester 1947**

4-6-0 (23)
  'Castle'      4086/92, 5017, 5063/92, 7005
  'Star'      4007/51
  'Hall'      4980, 5914/7/83, 6916/21/30/6/8/47/50/1
  'Grange'      6807/51/77

4-4-0 (3)
  'Bulldog'      3382/93, 3440

2-8-0 (5)
  'ROD'      3021/7/9/30/48

2-6-0 (8)
  '43xx'      6306/24/78/82/5/96, 7301/8

0-6-0 (16)
  '2301'      2339, 2458, 2551
  '2251'      2205/7/37/41/2/7/63/75/7/8/90/4

2-6-2T (12)
  '45xx'      4504/46/58
  '4575'      4596, 5544
  '51xx'      5112/4
  '5101'      4100/14/39, 5173
  '81xx'      8106

0-6-0T (20)
  '850'      1919, 2001/7/16
            2007 saddle tank
  '2021'      2037/51, 2100/1/15
  '2721'      2743/99
  '57xx'      3607/4613/4/29/41/64, 7750
  '74xx'      7416

0-4-2T
  '3571'      3574
  '48xx'      1408/18, 5816/6

*Total 93*

Diesel railcars (7) 5, 6, 7, 14, 22/7, 31
Sub sheds:
  Evesham      0-6-0 PT 2774
  Honeybourne and Kingham — no engines allocated

**Hereford 1938**

4-6-0 (7)
   'Saint'       2921/80
   'Hall'        4913/52/74/7, 5965
4-4-0 (3)
   'Bulldog'   3316, 3409/32
2-6-0 (5)
   '26xx'      2680
   '43xx'      4302, 5345/77, 6389
0-6-0 (2)
   '2301'      2325, 2471
2-6-2T (1)
   '45xx'      4560
0-6-0T (14)
   '850'       1989, 2020
   '2021'      2024/5, 3131/8
   '1501'      1509/38
   '655'       1746
   '57xx'      3725, 7707, 8781
   '74xx'      7416
0-4-2T (2)
   '48xx'      4802/6

*Total 34*

Sub sheds:
   Ledbury      One 0-6-0T, usually '75xx'
   Ross-on-Wye  One auto engine ('84xx'), one 0-6-0PT


**112**

No 4327 stands beside the coal stack at Worcester shed in 1932. *J. A. G. H. Coltas*

112

**Hereford 1947**

4-6-0 (12)
   'Castle'    4079
   'Saint'     2920/4/32/7/44/8/51/87
   'Hall'      6905/20/43
4-4-0 (2)
   'Bulldog'   3432/54
2-8-0 (1)
   '28xx'      2807
2-6-0 (7)
   '26xx'      2651/80
   '43xx'      5348/77, 6349/52/95
0-6-0 (5)
   '2301'      2349, 2541
   '2251'      2243/86, 3209
2-6-2T (1)
   'ADR'      1206
0-6-0T (19)
   '2021'      2026/9/40/96, 2102/38
   '57xx'      3601, 3725/8/89, 4600/57/78, 5765, 7707, 9619
   '655'       2714
   '74xx'      7420
0-4-2T (8)
   '14xx'      1404/45/55/60, 5807/8/14/7

*Total 55*

Sub sheds:
   Leominster   0-6-0PT 2714; 0-4-2T 5807/17
   Kington     0-4-2T 5808/14
   Ledbury     0-6-0PT 3725/8
   Ross-on-Wye  0-6-0PT 7420; 0-4-2T 1404/45

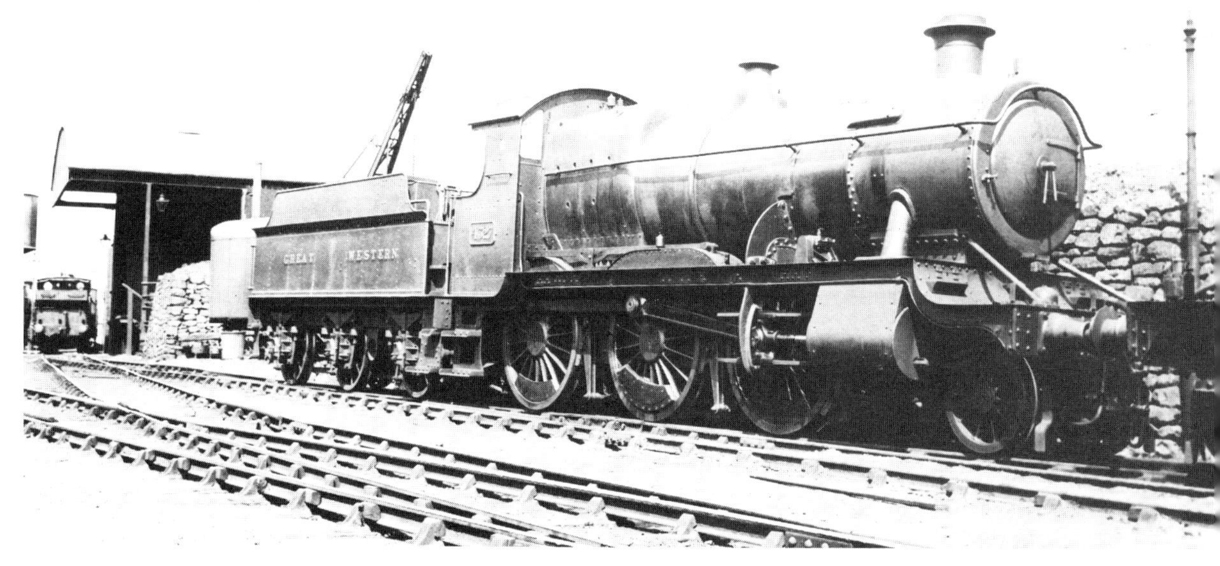

**Kidderminster 1938**

0-6-0 (1)
   '2251'       2286
2-6-2T (7)
   '4575'       4586/94/6, 5515/44/74
   '51xx'       5112
0-6-0T (7)
   '850'        2001
   '64xx'       6430
   '57xx'       8718/27/31
   'CMDP'     28/9

*Total 16*

No sub sheds

**Kidderminster 1947**

2-6-0 (1)
   '43xx'       5303
2-6-2T (8)
   '4575'       4584/6/94, 5518/73
   '5101'       4133, 5110
   '81xx'       8101
0-6-0T (7)
   '2021'       2093
   '57xx'       4625, 4770, 8718/27
   'CMDP'     28/9

*Total 16*

No sub sheds

**113**

**113**
Minus connecting and coupling rods, No 5375 is under repair outside the Worcester repair shops in 1932. *J. A. G. H. Coltas*

**114**

**114**
Until a new shed was opened in 1932, Kidderminster's facilities were both primitive and limited. Coaling was done direct from wagons under a small shelter. Ex-LMM 0-6-0T No 803 was on loan to Kidderminster, for working the CMDP line while No 28 was being rebuilt during 1931. *J. A. G. H. Coltas*

110

117

**116**

Inside the new shed at Stourbridge. 0-6-0ST No 2108 still carries the domeless boiler with which it was built in 1902. It lost both its saddle tank and domeless boiler in 1934. 24 April 1932. *W. Potter*

**117**

As Hereford's repair shop did not possess a wheel drop, LNER 'J25' class 0-6-0 No 2072, on loan to the GWR, has been raised by means of the hoist. 23 November 1940. *R. C. Riley*

**118**

Evesham's small sub-shed normally had only one engine allocated to it. However, on 24 April 1956, no less than three are in evidence. The lines in the foreground are those of the LMS Redditch to Ashchurch branch. *R. C. Riley*

**Stourbridge 1938**

2-6-0 (7)
  '26xx'    2608/20/3/55
  '43xx'    5346, 6346/90

0-6-0 (7)
  '2301'    2320/89, 2413/51, 2513/38/60

2-6-2T (22)
  '5101'    5101/5/6/7/51/2/65/8/79/93/6/7
  '51xx'    5121/2/31/5/9/41/4/5/7/9

0-6-0T (31)
  '2021'    2104/7/9/10/47/52/6
  '655'    1742/8/76/80/7/8, 2706/12/6/9
  '1854'    1863
  '2721'    3777
  '57xx'    5791/5, 6748, 8705/29/87, 9728/74/94
  '64xx'    6405/18

0-4-2T (4)
  '48xx'    4819/38/53/7

*Total 71*

No sub sheds


### 115

Stourbridge old shed dated from 1870 and was
replaced by a new building in 1926, after which it was
used to stable steam railmotors and later diesel
railcars. Nos 40 and 93 of the former class stand
outside. 24 April 1932. *W. Potter*

115

**Stourbridge 1947**

4-4-0 (2)
  'Bulldog'    3450
  'Duke'    9084

2-8-0 (1)
  '28xx'    2852

2-6-0 (2)
  '26xx'    2620/55

0-6-0 (4)
  '2251'    2246/70/9/81

2-6-2T (26)
  '5101'    4104/46/9/50, 5101/5/7/55/60/5/7/70/80/9/91/3/6/7
  '51xx'    5122/31/4/6/8/41/6/7

0-6-2T (8)
  '56xx'    6617/46/65/7/74/7/8/84

0-6-0T (36)
  '655'    1745/9, 2706/12
  '1813'    1835
  '2721'    2771
  '2021'    2090/2, 2107
  '2181'*    2185/6/7/9

0-4-2T (3)
  '48xx'    1410/4/38

*Total 82*

Diesel railcars (2) 8, 33
No sub sheds
* '2181' class were '2021' class with improved braking
power